The Sun's Family

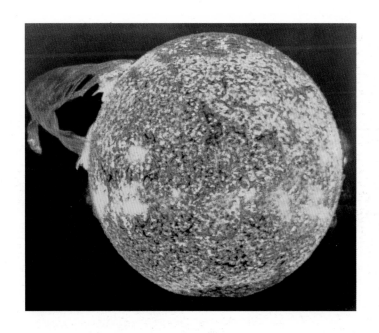

VOLUME 1
OUTER●SPACE

The Sun's Family

Robert Hitt, Jr.

Grolier Educational

SHERMAN TURNPIKE, DANBURY, CONNECTICUT 06816

Published 1998 by Grolier Educational
Danbury, Connecticut 06816

Michael Friedman Publishing Group, Inc.
Editors: Susan Lauzau, Nathaniel Marunas,
and Celeste Sollod
Art Director: Jeff Batzli
Designers: Elan Studio, Devorah Wolf,
and Lynne Yeamans
Photography Editors: Karen Barr and Deidra Gorgos
Illustration Art Direction: Deidra Gorgos

Published by arrangement with
Michael Friedman Publishing Group, Inc.
15 West 26th Street
New York, NY 10010

Library of Congress Cataloging in Publication Data

Outer space.
      p.   cm.
    Includes bibliographical references and index.
    Contents: v. 1. The sun's family — v. 2. The moon — v. 3. The
inner planets — v. 4. The outer planets — v. 5. The night sky —
v. 6. Stars and galaxies — v. 7. Astronomy — v. 8. Space travel -
v. 9. Space Shuttle — v. 10. Astronauts and cosmonauts — v.
11. Space stations — v. 12. Satellites and probes.
    ISBN 0-7172-9179-0 (set)
    1. Astronomy—Juvenile literature. 2. Outer space—Juvenile
literature. 3. Astronautics—Juvenile literature. [1. Astronomy.
2. Outer space. 3. Astronautics.]   I. Grolier Educational (Firm)
QB46.0826   1998
520—DC21   97-49010

First Edition
Printed in England

Photo Credits

Corbis-Bettmann: pp. 13, 14, 28 bottom, 35 bottom, 43
both, 44 top; ©Jay Pasachoff: pp. 34 left, 35 top

Lloyd Birmingham: Illustrations: pp. 8 bottom, 9 both,
10, 15

©Ken Blackwell: pp. 38 bottom, 41

FPG International: ©Laurence B. Aiuppy: p. 2

Greg Harris: Illustrations: pp. 30, 31, 47

Courtesy Library of Congress: p. 12

NASA: pp. 1, 5 both, 8 top, 16, 17 bottom, 19, 21, 22 top,
23 top, 26 both, 28 top, 29, 33 right, 34 right, 42, 44
bottom, 46, 49, 50, 51 both, 52-53

Tom Stack and Associates: Airworks: p. 38 top;
Airworks/USNO: p. 40; ©Thomas Kitchin: p. 33 left;
NASA/GSFS: p. 18 bottom; NASA/Hubble/Airworks: p. 11
bottom; NASA/JPL: pp. 22 bottom, 24, 25;
NASA/JPL/TSADO: pp. 6–7, 23 bottom; NASA/TSADO:
p. 32; NOAA: p. 36; TSADO/JPL: pp. 7 right, 17 top, 18
top, 48; TSADO/ NOAO: pp. 27, 37 top, 39;
TSADO/USGS: p. 20 both

©UC Regents/UCO Lick Observatory: pp. 11 top,
37 bottom

UPI/Corbis Bettmann: p. 45

CONTENTS

INTRODUCTION

We live in a space community known as the **solar system**, a term that refers to our Sun and its family, which includes the planets and billions of lesser-known objects that are all affected by the Sun's gravity. In fact, astronomers continue to debate the size of the Sun's family. It is not clear how many objects orbit the Sun, or how far the Sun's gravity reaches out into space. A few people consider the orbit of Pluto as the edge of the solar system, but that may not be accurate. The Pioneer and Voyager **(Vol. 12, pp. 52–53)** spacecraft have traveled beyond the orbit of Pluto and are redefining our perspective on the size and nature of the Sun's family. The Sun's gravity may reach out billions of miles beyond the orbits of the planets.

In this book we will explore how astronomers think the solar system was born and discuss the orbits of the planets. We will examine how the Sun produces its energy and why it has spots on its outer gas clouds. Why are some planets solid

This photograph of the surface of the Sun was captured using special film and shows the incredible amount of activity that occurs there; in the Sun's upper atmosphere, known as the chromosphere, gases swirl and temperatures exceed 1 million degrees Fahrenheit (555, 538°C).

and others just gas? What are the planets known as the gas giants **(pp. 21–25)** like inside? The book will also explain the awesome sight of the Moon passing in front of the Sun, which is what causes a solar eclipse **(pp. 33–36)**. Why do some Earthbound observers see a total eclipse while others do not see it at all? We will examine such visitors to our skies as comets **(pp. 37–42)** and asteroids **(pp. 46–49)**, which the Sun's gravity pulls in from outer space. We will explore meteor craters and consider the possibility that Earth might one day be destroyed by a killer asteroid. And we will examine the outer reaches of the Sun's gravitational field and consider whether or not there might be an undiscovered planet out there.

◄

Command module of the Pioneer IV spacecraft, which sent loads of data about the universe back to Earth during its mission.

THE BIRTH OF THE SOLAR SYSTEM

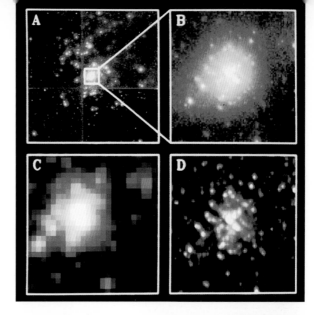

Current scientific theory suggests that approximately five billion years ago the Sun and planets were formed in a large cloud of dust and gas. This gas cloud, or **nebula**, was made up mostly of **hydrogen**, the most abundant type of gas in the universe. In the beginning some unknown force caused a disturbance in the nebula, and the force of **gravity** (a force of attraction that exists between all objects with mass) began to pull each **atom** of gas in the nebula toward the center of the cloud. As the nebula collapsed, the internal pressures of the cloud began to increase. This caused great amounts of energy to be released, and the nebula slowly started to spin, or **rotate**.

▼
This illustration shows the spinning nebula that would eventually become the solar system slowly rotating as gravity pulls the gases together. The central part of the nebula became the Sun, and the outer layers became the planets and other members of the solar system.

The Sun

In the center of the nebula a large gas sphere began to form that would eventually become a star. (This process is known as **gravitational collapse**, and once it starts, it will not stop until some force acts to stop the gases from rushing in.)

▲
Portrait of a young nebula: (A,B,D) are of the nebula known as 30 Doradus, 160,000 light years from Earth, taken by the Hubble Space Telescope (HST) **[Vol. 7, pp. 37–44]**. (C) was taken by a large Earth-based telescope. (A) is a wide field/planetary camera view of the nebula. (B) is an enlargement of the central portion of the nebula showing compact star cluster R136, of very hot and massive young stars. (C) is another view of the same region as (B). (D) is a computer-enhanced version of (B) showing the young individual stars inside the nebula.

High pressures inside the newly forming star caused atoms of gas to react with each other. Hydrogen atoms began to react with other

The Planets and Moons

The combination of the gases moving in and around the Sun and the outward pressure of its energy produced zones, or layers, within the remaining nebula. Small currents and eddies in these layers developed into large pockets of gas and dust. These pockets of gas and dust began to condense and slowly develop into spinning, **denser objects** that are now called **planets**. Smaller pockets of material began to form into **moons**.

▲

Eddies of material from the spinning nebula coalesce in orbit around the developing Sun, becoming planets. The Sun and planets spin due to the conservation of energy within the nebula.

▼

The new planets continue to form as they are pulled around the Sun by gravity. In similar fashion matter spinning around the planets probably comes together to become the moons.

hydrogen atoms to form other kinds of atoms. The new atoms were of a gas known as **helium**. This process of atoms combining together is called **nuclear fusion (p. 28)**. The fusion process produces tremendous amounts of energy, enough to resist gravitational collapse and cause the nebula to stop shrinking. At the center of what had once been a giant cloud of gas and dust shone a star, the Sun.

The Sun continues to produce energy from the reactions of its gases. Each day the Sun consumes part of itself, converting millions of tons of hydrogen atoms into energy. Scientists say there is no need to worry about the Sun running out of gases any time soon: it is predicted that the Sun has enough hydrogen to last another five to ten billion years.

Where Did All the Mass Go?

Most of the **mass** (the amount of matter in an object and not its weight, which varies depending on the amount of gravity affecting the object) in our solar system is a mixture of gases, and the Sun contains 99.9 percent of that mass. Its estimated mass is 2.18 x 10^{27} tons (1.98 x 10^{30}kg). Most of the remaining mass of our solar system is accounted for by the **gas giants**, planets that are made up entirely (so far as is known) of gases. The gas giants are the planets Jupiter, Saturn, Uranus, and Neptune **(Vol. 4, pp. 16–45)**. The solid planets—Venus, Earth, Mars, and Mercury **(Vol. 3, pp. 21–46)**—and all the moons account for a tiny fraction of the mass of the solar system. Finally, the billions of smaller objects in our solar system—such as meteoroids, asteroids, and comets—have so little mass as to be negligible.

Other Nebulae, Other Solar Systems

Many other nebulae can be seen by astronomers observing the universe with large telescopes located on Earth and in space. Inside these nebulae new stars are forming. It is possible that millions of years in the future, some of these nebulae will develop into solar

◄

The solar system is born: the Sun's family includes one star (the Sun) along with planets, moons, and billions of comets, asteroids, and meteoroids.

The North American Nebula, so-called because it resembles the continent of North America in its shape, is in the constellation Cygnus and contains enough gases to form millions of new stars.

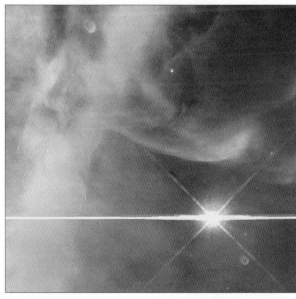

◄

Detail of the Orion Nebula in the constellation Orion. This nebula is illuminated by many nearby young stars. Scientists predict that this nebula has enough gases to form more than ten thousand stars with the mass of our Sun.

systems much like our own. Other stars with planets have already been identified. Evidence of other solar systems includes a star known as 51 Pegasi, which was discovered in the **constellation** Pegasus **(Vol. 5, p. 50)**. Scientists believe that this star is orbited by several planets, but they cannot tell much about them. Other planets have also been found around stars in the constellations of Virgo, Cygnus, and Ursa Major. Many of these planets are believed to be large gaseous planets, but there might be some **terrestrial** ("Earthlike") planets out there as well. The universe probably contains billions of other solar systems. All the atoms that make up our solar system were forged in the furnace of the Sun. This means that the atoms in our bodies were once part of a star.

THE PLANETS AND THEIR ORBITS

The earliest civilizations on Earth noticed several objects wandering the sky against the background of stars. The ancient Greeks named these objects *planets*, meaning "wanderers." There were only five known planets at the time because only four other planets were visible without the aid of a telescope. Today these planets are known by their Roman names: Mercury, Venus, Mars, Jupiter, and Saturn. Early astronomers did not understand that the planets moved around the Sun. The first astronomers thought the planets (and the Sun and the Moon) moved in perfect circles around Earth. A second-century Greek scholar named Claudius Ptolemy **(Vol. 7, p. 13)** improved this **geocentric** ("Earth-centered") theory, which remained popular for more than fifteen hundred years before the modern concept of the planets orbiting the Sun became popular **(Vol. 7, pp. 14–15)**.

Orbit Tilts

The planets do not orbit the Sun in perfectly circular **orbits**, or paths; instead, their orbits are ellipses. An **ellipse** is an elongated circle. This means that a planet's distance from the Sun changes depending on what position in the orbit the planet is in. The planet with the most elongated orbit is Pluto, and the planet with the least elongated orbit is Venus.

The planets do not orbit the Sun in the same orbit plane, or **ecliptic**. You might define the plane of the solar system with a line drawn between the center of Earth and the Sun; as Earth orbits the Sun, that line describes a flat surface, or **plane**. That plane is the ecliptic. Think of the planets as marbles on the surface of a table with the Sun in the center. In this model the surface of the table represents the ecliptic. All planet orbits are measured in reference to this

Early astronomers noticed the phasing of the Moon as it moved across the sky, as shown in this old French chart. Later, Galileo noticed that the planet Venus also displayed phases, suggesting it was in orbit around the Sun and contradicting the then-popular theory that all celestial bodies orbited the Earth.

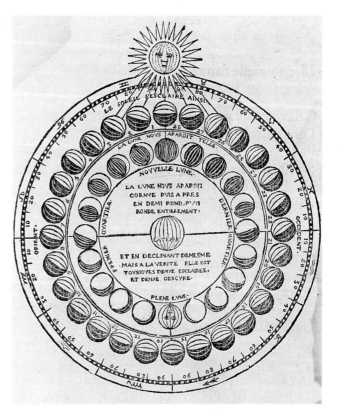

ORBIT TILTS

Planet	Orbit Tilt
Mercury	7.0 degrees
Venus	3.4 degrees
Earth	0.0 degrees
Mars	1.8 degrees
Jupiter	1.3 degrees
Saturn	2.5 degrees
Uranus	0.8 degrees
Neptune	1.8 degrees
Pluto	17.2 degrees

surface. Most are moving around the Sun very close to the ecliptic. Their orbits are tilted only a few degrees off the ecliptic. Pluto has the greatest orbit tilt, of 17.2 degrees above and below the ecliptic. The planet Uranus has the smallest orbit tilt—only 0.8 degrees, almost directly on the ecliptic.

Orbit Speeds

At present there are only nine known planets orbiting the Sun. The planets closest to the Sun are moving faster than those farther away. A planet's speed in orbit is a result of a delicate balance between the gravitational pull of the Sun and the planet's mass resisting this pull as it orbits the Sun. In order for a planet not to be pulled into the Sun, it must generate an outward push equal to the Sun's inward pull. This outward push of a planet is referred to as **centrifugal force** and is a result of the planet's motion. If the planets did not move,

there would be nothing stopping them from falling into the Sun.

As the planets move around the Sun, their orbit speeds are constantly changing. This motion was studied and observed by the astronomer Tycho Brahe (1546–1601) **(Vol. 5, p. 15)** around 1576. Brahe was not aware of elliptical orbits, but he made careful

▼

Tycho Brahe in his observatory on the island of Hven in 1602. The large curved instrument was used to measure the angles of elevation of celestial objects. Brahe's remarkably accurate measurements enabled such subsequent astronomers as Johannes Kepler to make additional discoveries about the Sun's family.

SCALE SIZE OF THE PLANETS

The Sun is so large that 109 Earths would fit across its diameter. If Earth were scaled down to the size of 1 inch (2.54cm) in diameter, the Sun would be 109 inches (276cm) in diameter. On that scale Pluto would be only 0.18 inch (45mm) in diameter. Below is a list of the scale diameter of the planets.

Object	Scale Diameter
Earth	1 inch (2.54cm)
Sun	109 inches (276cm)
Mercury	0.38 inch (93mm)
Venus	0.94 inch (2.38cm)
Earth	1 inch (2.54cm)
Mars	0.53 inch (1.35cm)
Jupiter	11.2 inches (28.4cm)
Saturn	9.44 inches (24cm)
Uranus	4 inches (10.2cm)
Neptune	3.88 inches (9.85cm)
Pluto	0.18 inches (45mm)

observations of the planets and recorded their movements for more than twenty years. It was the work of Brahe that enabled Johannes Kepler (1571–1630) to develop his three **laws of planetary motion (Vol. 5, pp. 16–17)** (between 1610 and 1619) and discover that the planets move in elliptical orbits.

Because the distance between a planet and the Sun is always changing depending on where the planet is in its orbit, the gravitational pull of the Sun on a planet changes as well. So as a planet gets closer to the Sun, its orbit speed increases due to the Sun's gravitational pull. When a planet is moving away from the Sun, its orbit speed lessens. Kepler did not know what was pulling the planets, but because he was a good observer and had access to the careful measurements of Brahe, his laws of planetary motion are among the most important discoveries in the history of science.

Mercury is the closest planet to the Sun and the swiftest planet in the solar system, traveling faster than 29 miles per second (48kps), or 107,000 miles per hour (172,800km/h). Mercury must travel fast, or the Sun's gravity will pull it into the Sun. (Mercury is difficult to see from Earth because the swift planet orbits so close to the Sun; it can only be observed just before sunrise or just after sunset, depending on its position around the Sun.) **(Vol. 3, pp. 21–24)**

AVERAGE DISTANCE OF THE PLANETS FROM THE SUN

Object	Average Distance from Sun (in millions of miles)
Mercury	36 (57.9 million km)
Venus	67 (108.2 million km)
Earth	93 (149.6 million km)
Mars	143 (228 million km)
Jupiter	483 (778 million km)
Saturn	887 (1,427 million km)
Uranus	1,783 (2,870 million km)
Neptune	2,794 (4,497 million km)
Pluto	3,666 (5,900 million km)

Pluto is the farthest planet from the Sun, so it is not strongly affected by the Sun's gravity. It takes Pluto more than 248 years to orbit the Sun. Pluto's orbit speed is slightly less than 3 miles per second (4.7km/s), or 10,500 miles per hour (17,000km/h). Pluto also has the strangest orbit of any planet. It has the greatest orbit tilt relative to the ecliptic and is off-center when compared with the other planets. Due to its extremely elliptical orbit, Pluto is sometimes closer to the Sun than is Neptune. It last crossed inside the orbit of Neptune in 1979. Pluto spends only a short time inside the orbit of Neptune—about

▼

The orbits of all the planets are ellipses, but Pluto's orbit is the most elliptical of all. One side of its orbit lies inside the orbit of Neptune, but there is no chance that Neptune and Pluto will ever collide because Pluto's orbit is tilted above the ecliptic.

CENTRIFUGAL FORCE IN ACTION

You can demonstrate centrifugal force by swinging a small object attached to a piece of string around your head. Think of the object as a planet, yourself as the Sun, and the string as the Sun's gravitational hold on the planet. The object orbiting your head seems to pull out against the string. This outward force is only generated when the object is moving. If you stop swinging the object, the outward force is lost, and the object falls inward. Think what would happen if a planet stopped moving around the Sun. What do you think would happen if the Sun's gravity no longer pulled on the planets?

twenty years of its 248-year-long orbit. There is no chance that Pluto and Neptune will collide since the two planets keep many millions of miles apart **(Vol. 4, pp. 49–51)**.

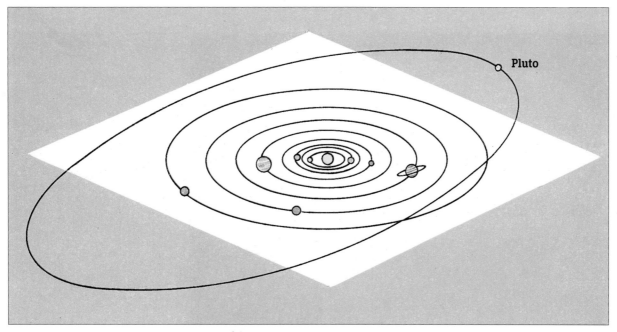

THE PLANETS AND THEIR ORBITS

TERRESTRIAL ("EARTHLIKE") PLANETS

The planets in the solar system are divided into two types, the terrestrial planets and the gas giants. The planets Mercury, Venus, Earth, and Mars are all considered terrestrial planets. The planet Pluto is also solid but is considered to be unusual because of its small size. All the terrestrial planets are located close to the Sun, inside the orbit of Jupiter **(p. 14)**. Even though these planets are referred to as Earthlike, they are not very similar to Earth. Their main similarity is in their solid surfaces. Some have a thin atmosphere, and some are shrouded with thick layers of poisonous gases. Humans could land a spacecraft on any of the terrestrial planets, but it would be impossible to live on them.

Mercury

The surface of the planet Mercury changes dramatically in temperature from hot to cold. In midday the planet is baked by the Sun and reaches temperatures of more than 800°F (470°C) and then drops to around -360°F (-180°C) at night. This is because Mercury has no **atmosphere** to protect it from the Sun's heat or the cold of space. Imagine the atmosphere of a planet to be its blanket. Mercury has no blanket to protect it from the Sun's heat during the day or keep it warm at night. In photos taken by the Mariner 10 spacecraft, the first to photograph the planet at close range, the surface of the planet turned out to be covered with **craters**. The surface looks much like the surface of our Moon. Most of the craters were created millions of years ago by large meteors and comets slamming into the planet's unprotected surface. Since Mercury has no weather

◄

This image of Mercury, revealing thousands of craters on its airless surface, was assembled from photographs taken by the Mariner 10 spacecraft on March 29, 1974.

(weather cannot occur without an atmosphere) to wash these scars away, they are still visible **(Vol. 3, pp. 21–24)**.

Venus

Venus is often considered the sister of Earth since they are roughly the same size, but humans could never live on Venus. Its layers of atmosphere are almost one hundred times thicker than the atmosphere of Earth, and as a result Venus's surface is the hottest of any planet in the solar system, baking in the Sun's heat. Scientists call this the **greenhouse effect (Vol. 3, p. 33)**. Sunlight and heat pass through the atmosphere of Venus and become trapped.

This is similar to the way a closed car heats up in the summer sun. Sunlight and heat are reflected off the interior of the car and warm the air inside, but this hot air cannot escape because the car doors and windows are closed. Similarly, the trapped heat of Venus cannot escape back through the atmosphere, and the

◄

This is a Hubble Space Telescope photograph of Venus taken on January 24, 1995. The polar regions appear as bright patches, possibly due to a haze of particles overlying the main clouds. Venus's clouds are made of sulfuric acid, rather than the water-vapor clouds of Earth, and travel east to west around the planet with the prevailing winds, circling the planet every four days. This image has been color-enhanced to highlight the cloud features.

◄

Computer image of Venus's surface made by the Magellan space-craft reveals extensive lava flows from past volcanic activity.

temperature rises dramatically. The entire surface of Venus is almost 1,000°F (500°C), and it is hot all the time. The best photos of Venus were taken by the Magellan spacecraft, which used a **radar-imaging (Vol. 12, pp. 29–30)** camera that could penetrate the thick atmosphere.

the Sun during the day and keeps them from freezing at night. It also filters out the Sun's harmful **ultraviolet** rays. Because the Earth's atmosphere, which is made up of mostly **nitrogen** and **oxygen (Vol. 3, p. 33)**, isn't as dense as Venus's, it doesn't trap as much

Earth

Earth is the only planet known to support life, and it is the only planet with liquid water. In fact, 72 percent of the planet is covered with oceans, seas, and other bodies of water. A unique feature of this planet is its life-supporting atmosphere, which protects organisms from the heat of

▶

The Earth is a mix of water, land, and atmosphere that is conducive to life as we know it. Here, the continents of North and South America are easily viewed along with the polar ice of Antarctica.

EARTH'S ATMOSPHERE

Earth's atmosphere is made up of 78 percent nitrogen, 20 percent oxygen, 1 percent water vapor, 0.93 percent argon, 0.03 percent carbon dioxide, and traces of other gases.

heat. Unlike the planets that lack an atmosphere, the surface of Earth is constantly changing. Like other terrestrial planets, Earth is cratered, but atmospheric storms generated by the heat of the Sun weather away our planet's surface in a process called **erosion**.

Mars

Mars is a small planet, only half the size of Earth, and has a very thin atmosphere (the air pressure is only about 7 percent that of Earth). Humans could never live on Mars. It has a solid surface but

This view of Earth's Grand Canyon was taken from the space shuttle. The Grand Canyon was formed by millions of years of erosion caused by the movement of water across the land surface. Similar features have been observed on Mars, suggesting that the Red Planet also once had water on its surface.

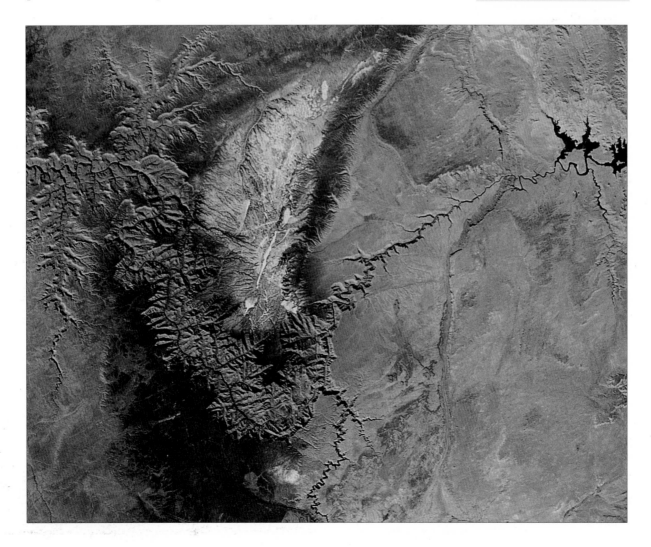

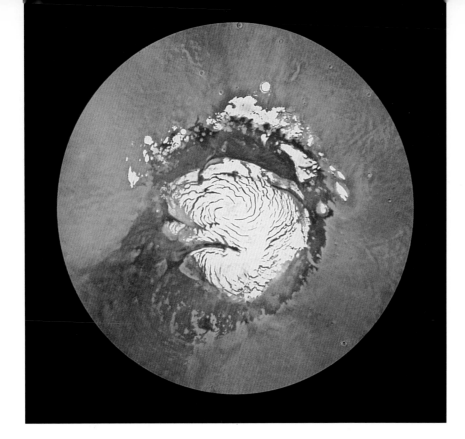

Mars has a polar ice cap made of frozen carbon dioxide gas. As the gases melt, they turn directly from a solid into a gas, skipping a liquid state. The polar ice caps become larger during the Martian winter and smaller during the Martian summer.

lacks breathable air and drinkable water. The planet's thin atmosphere makes it easy to observe its surface from Earth. Many years ago some astronomers thought there was life on Mars. The American astronomer Percival Lowell (1855–1916) made a lifelong study of Mars **(Vol. 3, p. 48)**. He observed the polar ice caps and dark markings on the surface, and was convinced that the dark patches were plants, and that the melting ice of the polar caps was allowing them to grow.

Excellent photos of Mars were taken by the Mariner and Viking spacecraft in the 1970s, and in 1997 the Pathfinder mission landed on the planet and deployed a remote-

The largest canyon system in the solar system, seen here, is found on Mars. It is over 2,000 miles (3,219km) long and appears to have been made by a flowing liquid (possibly water).

controlled vehicle to survey the surface. Later in 1997 the Mars Global Surveyor went into orbit around the Red Planet in order to photograph its entire surface **(Vol. 12, pp. 47–49)**. Of all the terrestrial planets, Mars is the one scientists want to send astronauts to first.

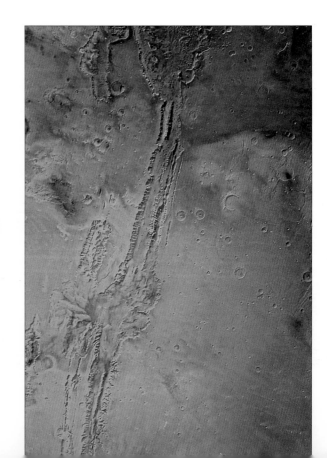

THE GAS GIANTS

The four largest planets in the solar system are called the gas giants. They are the planets Jupiter, Saturn, Uranus, and Neptune, and they contain most of the mass of the solar system not accounted for by the Sun. The region of the solar system these planets occupy is very different from that occupied by the terrestrial planets since the region occupied by the gas giants is far from the Sun, where it is darker and colder. All the gas giants have rings made of ice and dust particles. The size of these ring particles ranges from microscopic specks to objects the size of large buildings. The gas giants also have many moons.

The gas giants have no observable solid surface. Because of the extreme cold the gases on these planets did not evaporate into space (leaving solids behind). Below the cloud tops observable from Earth there is possibly a layer of liquid hydrogen, followed by a layer of metallic hydrogen. At the center there might be a liquid or solid core (no one knows for sure which). It would be impossible to land a spacecraft on any of these planets. The gas giants are often called **Jovian** ("Jupiterlike") planets because they are made of gases and resemble Jupiter.

MOON COUNT

Planet	Number of Moons
Mercury	0
Venus	0
Earth	1
Mars	2
Jupiter	16
Saturn	18
Uranus	15
Neptune	8
Pluto	1

◄

Saturn and its ring system are clearly visible in this HST photograph. The stripes in its atmosphere are a result of the planet's fast spin. The gases with the greater density form layers near the planet's equator. The material in the rings might be the remains of a moon pulled apart by Saturn's gravity.

Jupiter

The largest of the gas giants is the planet Jupiter, which has more than 318 times the mass of Earth. Jupiter's diameter is 88,980 miles (142,980km). It is so large that if it were hollow over twelve hundred Earths would fit inside it. The observable surface of Jupiter is made of layers of hydrogen, helium, and traces of other gases such as ammonia and methane. The striped appearance is caused by solar-driven winds and the spin of the planet. The denser gases move toward the planet's equator. There are also **convection currents** of gas rising to the visible surface, then falling again toward the center. Scientists believe that the rising gases appear lighter than the descending gases. The different colors are a result of the different gases reflecting sunlight.

Jupiter's most famous feature is the **great red spot**. This spot is a mystery. It appears to be a spinning storm more than 30,000 miles (48,270km) long and 8,700 miles (14,000km) wide that could easily hold several Earths. Its size and color change for some unknown reason. It is possibly a large **high-pressure area** trapped in the planet's quickly spinning atmosphere. Scientists believe the red spot has existed for thousands of years; it has been viewed by astronomers for more than three hundred years. The first person ever to see the great red spot was the English astronomer Robert Hooke (1635–1703) **(Vol. 4, pp. 16–31)**.

▶

Jupiter's moon Io displays a mysterious bright spot in this photograph taken by the HST, July 1995. The spot might represent super-hot lava from the volcano Ra Patera, which was first photographed by Voyager 2 in 1979.

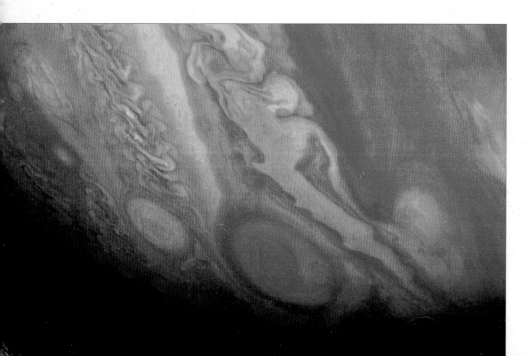

◀

Jupiter's great red spot is possibly a mixture of gases trapped in the planet's rotating atmosphere. This photograph was taken by the Voyager spacecraft.

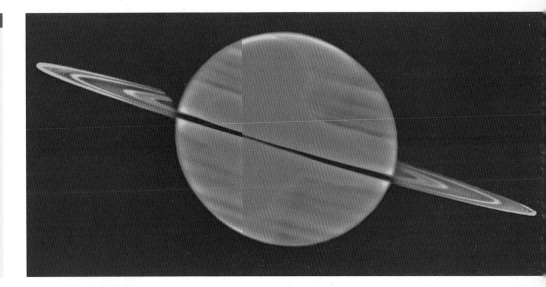

Saturn

Saturn is considered by some people to be the most beautiful planet in the solar system. It appears as a pale yellow object against the night sky, its yellow color caused by sunlight reflecting off its **ammonia** atmosphere. The second-largest of the gas giants, with a mass equal to that of ninety-five Earths, Saturn, like Jupiter, appears to have a striped surface. Spots are also visible in the cloud belts, but they are not as large at the spots on Jupiter. Saturn is famous for its rings. For many years it was the only planet known to have rings,

but it has since been discovered that all the gas planets have rings. In 1977 scientists discovered rings around Uranus, in 1979 rings were discovered around Jupiter, and finally in 1989 rings were discovered around Neptune. You can see Saturn's rings

SATURN'S RINGS "DISAPPEAR"

Saturn is tilted on its axis as it orbits the Sun. Once every fifteen years the rings of Saturn are turned edge-on to Earth and cannot be observed. The rings will face Earth in this way again in the year 2010

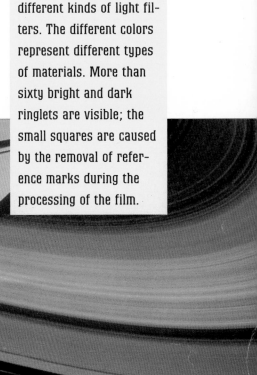

This false-color image of Saturn's C-ring and B-ring was photographed by Voyager 2 using three different kinds of light filters. The different colors represent different types of materials. More than sixty bright and dark ringlets are visible; the small squares are caused by the removal of reference marks during the processing of the film.

though a low-power telescope **(Vol. 4, pp. 35–36)**. The first person to observe Saturn's rings was Italian astronomer Galileo Galilei (1564–1642) **(Vol. 5, pp. 17–18)** in 1610, but he did not understand what he was seeing. In 1659 Christian Huygens (1629–95) in the Netherlands correctly identified "rings" around Saturn **(Vol. 4, pp. 32–39)**.

Uranus

The planet Uranus appears green when observed through a telescope. The atmosphere contains large amounts of methane, hydrogen, and helium gas. The third-largest of the gas giants, its mass is fourteen times that of Earth. The strangest thing about this gas giant is the fact that it rotates on its side. Uranus's axis is

AXIS TILT OF PLANETS

Planet	Axis Tilt
Mercury	0.0 degrees
Venus	177.4 degrees
Earth	23.4 degrees
Mars	25.2 degrees
Jupiter	3.1 degrees
Saturn	25.3 degrees
Uranus	97.9 degrees
Neptune	28.3 degrees
Pluto	123.0 degrees

Note: Because Venus, Uranus, and Pluto rotate backward (that is, in **retrograde** fashion), north poles are considered to be positioned below the ecliptic; as a result, their axis tilts are measured at greater than 90 degrees.

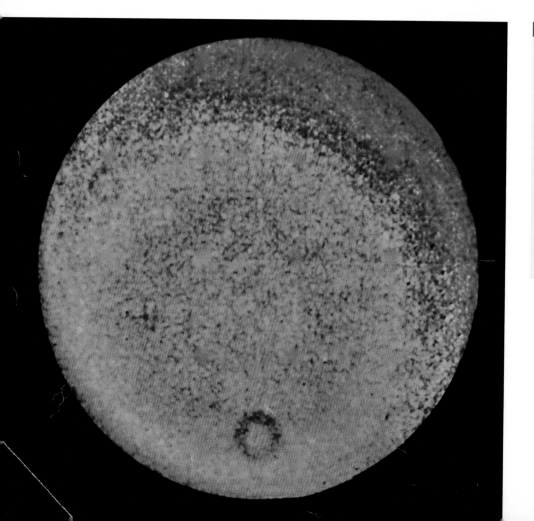

◄

Uranus appears feature-less in this Voyager 2 image. The green-blue color is due to the planet's methane atmo-sphere. The axis of the planet is practically par-allel to the ecliptic, mak-ing the planet appear to "roll" around the Sun.

tilted 97.9 degrees and actually makes the planet upside-down with regard to the ecliptic. Uranus takes eighty-four years to orbit the Sun. Each pole faces the Sun for forty-two years. The south pole of Uranus will face the Sun until 2006; then the north pole will face the sun until 2048 **(Vol. 4, pp. 40–44)**.

Neptune

Neptune appears blue due to its **methane** atmosphere. It is the smallest of the gas giants and the most difficult to see from Earth. Neptune has a higher density than Uranus; its mass is seventeen times that of Earth. Neptune is far from the Sun, and its temperature is estimated to be –392°F (–200°C). From Neptune the Sun would appear as a small, bright star in a black sky. Neptune takes 165 years to orbit the Sun. Astronomers discovered this planet in 1846 by observing the planet Uranus. They noticed that something besides the Sun's gravity pulls on Uranus, making its orbit speed change. Neptune was the last known planet in the solar system until the discovery of Pluto eighty-four years later **(Vol. 4, pp. 45–48)**.

SIZE OF THE GAS GIANTS

Planet	Diameter
Jupiter	88,844 miles (142,980km)
Saturn	74,900 miles (120,540km)
Uranus	31,765 miles (51,120km)
Neptune	30,777 miles (49,530km)

PLUTO

The planet Pluto is something of a mystery. Although it is believed to be solid like the terrestrial planets, its tiny size makes it more like a moon. Some astronomers think it once was a moon of Neptune, but no proof of this exists. From Pluto the Sun would appear as a bright point of light (instead of a yellow disk) in a black starry sky. The moon Charon was discovered orbiting Pluto in 1978 and was named after the boatman who served Pluto, the Greek mythological god of the underworld. Astronomers believe the surface of Pluto must be frozen due to the extreme cold at Pluto's distance from the Sun. Temperatures are estimated to be a few degrees above **absolute zero**, the point at which there is no heat at all, and

molecules completely stop moving. The planet's **axis of rotation** is also believed to be tilted almost 90 degrees in relation to its orbit plane. In 1988 astronomers observed Pluto **occulting**, or passing in front of, a dim star in the constellation Virgo. The star's light seemed to dim as Pluto blocked it from Earth's view. This dimming effect suggests that Pluto might have a thin atmosphere, probably made of methane gas; if Pluto had no atmosphere at all, the light from the star would simply wink out when Pluto occulted it **(Vol. 4, pp. 49–51)**.

◄
Pluto's great distance from Earth prevented ground-based telescopes on Earth from capturing a clear photo of its moon, Charon (left). Unobstructed by any atmosphere, the Earth-orbiting Hubble Space Telescope was able to photograph the moon clearly (right).

◄
This is the first image ever taken of Pluto's surface. The light and dark areas are possibly due to such topographic features as basins and craters. The image was taken by the European Space Agency's Faint Object Camera aboard the Hubble Space Telescope. The map covers 85 percent of the planet's surface.

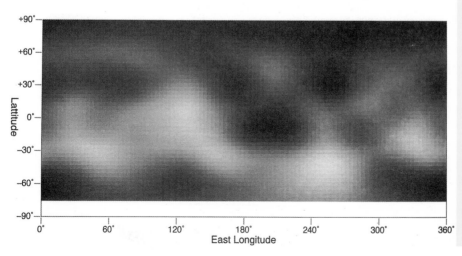

OUR STAR, THE SUN

ASTRONOMICAL UNIT

One astronomical unit is the average distance between Earth and the Sun. 1 AU = 92,955,806 miles (149,597,870km)

One of Earth's next-door neighbors is a star, the Sun. It appears large from Earth because it is the closest star to Earth, with an average distance of almost 93 million miles (150 million km). This distance is sometimes referred to as an **astronomical unit (AU) [see sidebar, this page]**.

The next-closest star to Earth is more than 26 trillion miles (41.8 trillion km) away. With a diameter of less than one million miles (1.4 million km), the Sun is not a large star relative to other stars. Some of the stars we see at night are millions of miles in diameter. The Sun is very large compared to the other members of our solar system; it accounts for more than 99.9 percent of all the mass in the entire system. The Sun's mass is more than 332,000 times the mass of Earth. In volume, one million Earths would fit inside the Sun.

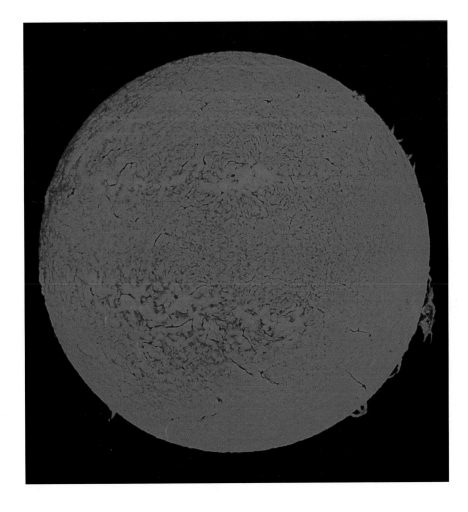

◄

This photograph of the Sun's surface, a kind of image called a spectroheliogram, shows all kinds of activity. Notice the solar prominence along the limb of the Sun.

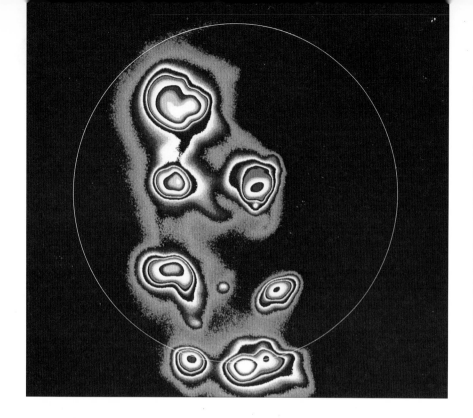

This X-ray image of the Sun's surface was taken by the Skylab space station in 1973. The image shows that solar activity, which occurs in eleven-year cycles, appears to be restricted to two parallel belts just to the north and south of the solar equator.

E=MC²

Albert Einstein was a theoretical physicist. Winner of the 1921 Nobel Prize for physics, he was one of the twentieth century's most profound investigators into the workings of the universe.

In this formula E is the energy released in the conversion of mass (m) during fusion; c is the speed of light (186,322 miles per second [298,115km/s]). Because the speed of light is a large number, when c is squared, it becomes a really huge number. Thus even a small amount of mass (m) produces a large amount of energy (E).

Fusion Power

The Sun does not "burn" like a fireplace. Instead, it produces energy through a process called nuclear fusion. In fusion the nuclei of atoms of lighter elements combine to make a heavier **nucleus**. In this process something strange happens: the amount of mass formed is less than the original mass of the combined elements. The missing mass is converted into energy. A small amount of mass creates a great amount of energy. The physicist Albert Einstein (1879–1955) created a mathematical expression stating how much energy would be released by fusion. His equation $E=mc^2$ relates mass to energy **(see sidebar on this page)**.

Using Einstein's formula, a mass weighing only one ton (970kg) would produce more energy through the process of fusion than the entire United States consumes (of all kinds) in one year. Scientists believe the

Sun is consuming its mass at the rate of 5 million tons (4.5 million metric tons, roughly the mass of more than one million automobiles) per second. At its current size the Sun has enough mass to last five to ten billion years or more. The energy produced at the center of the Sun takes a long time to reach the surface. The energy reaching Earth today was generated more than 30,000 years ago inside the Sun's core.

The Layers of the Sun

The surface of the Sun is actually a thin layer of gases called the **photosphere**. The temperature here is about 11,000°F (6,000°C). Deeper inside the Sun the temperature rises due to the increase in pressure. At the Sun's core it is more than 59 million°F (15 million°C). Above the photosphere is a thin layer called the **chromosphere**. During a solar eclipse the chromosphere appears to be brilliant hot pink.

SPECTRUM OF THE SUN

The light we see (the visible **spectrum**) is only a small part of the energy known as **electromagnetic energy**. It travels in the form of waves; the distance between these waves is called the **wavelength**. Some wavelengths are perceived by the human eye as colors. When sunlight passes through a **prism**, a rainbow of colors is released—this is the visible electromagnetic spectrum. The red colors are long wavelengths, and the blue are short.

This color is caused by the emission of hydrogen in the Sun's spectrum.

The outer gas layer of the Sun is called the **corona**. It is visible during a total solar eclipse. In this region of the Sun the temperatures are hotter than in the photosphere.

The Sun will continue to generate heat for billions of years. When most of its hydrogen has been fused into helium, the Sun will

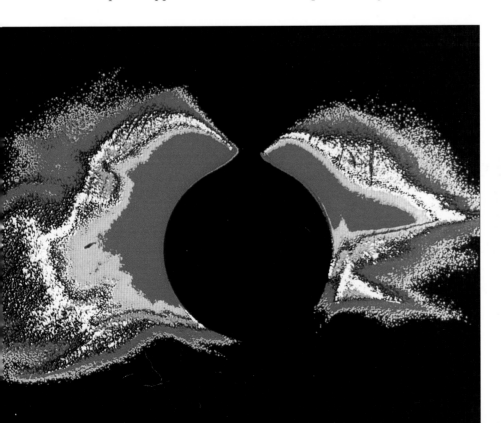

◄

Taken by the Skylab Space Station in 1974, this image of the corona (the Sun's hot outer atmosphere) has been color-coded to show different levels of brightness. The corona extends outward from the Sun for millions of miles in every direction.

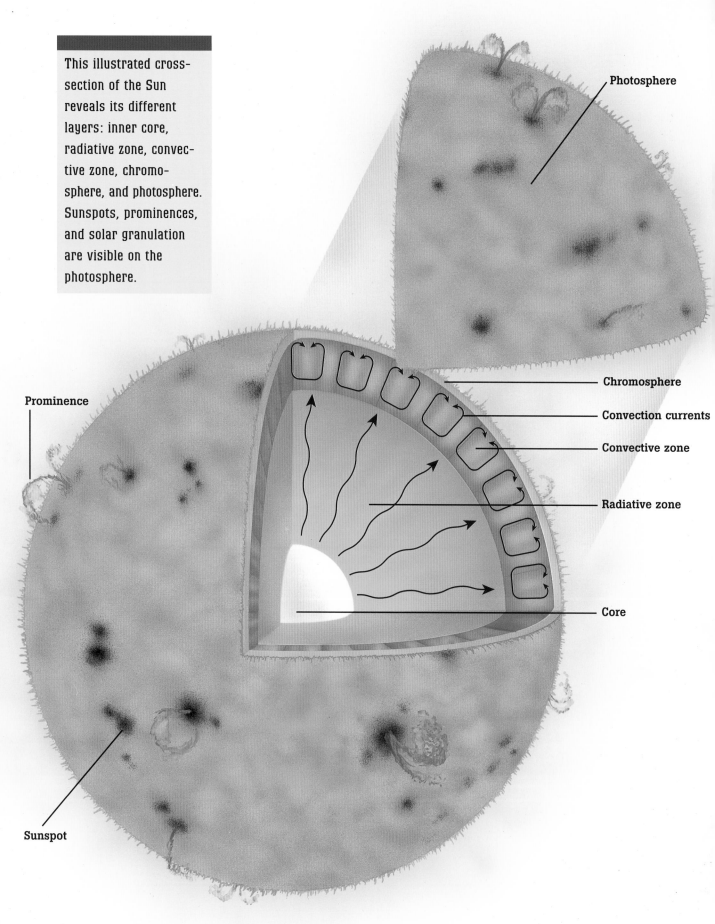

This illustrated cross-section of the Sun reveals its different layers: inner core, radiative zone, convective zone, chromosphere, and photosphere. Sunspots, prominences, and solar granulation are visible on the photosphere.

Photosphere

Chromosphere

Convection currents

Convective zone

Radiative zone

Core

Prominence

Sunspot

OUR STAR, THE SUN

------

begin to shrink. This will cause an increase in temperature and temporarily reheat the core. This in turn will cause the Sun to expand and become a **red giant** star. Its diameter will possibly expand beyond the orbit of Venus, and it will remain a red giant for millions of years before cooling down and becoming a **white dwarf (Vol. 6, pp. 23–25)** the size of Earth. As a white dwarf it will no longer produce thermonuclear reactions. When it finally radiates its last heat into space, it will become a **black dwarf**—a cold, dead star.

▼

This illustration shows the Sun as a red giant. After the Sun has consumed a certain portion of its mass, it will begin to shrink; this will in turn cause the core to reheat and then rapidly expand. This process will transform the Sun into a red giant, possibly larger than the orbits of Mercury, Venus, and Earth.

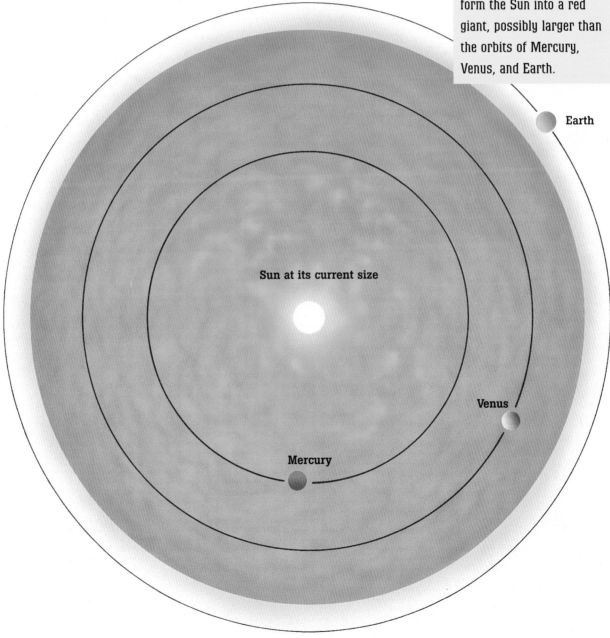

Earth

Sun at its current size

Venus

Mercury

Sunspots, Magnetic Storms, Solar Wind, and Solar Flares

The photosphere of the Sun appears smooth, but on closer inspection it turns out to have an "orange peel" texture. This textured appearance is due to the many small solar granules that appear on the surface. (Though small in relation to the size of the Sun, **solar granules** are hundreds of miles across.) Solar granules are actually hot blobs of gas rising to the surface of the Sun, where they release energy, cool, and sink back down (much like boiling liquid).

Sometimes the surface of the Sun has spots called **sunspots**, which are storms in the Sun's photosphere associated with the Sun's **magnetic field**. Sunspots appear dark because they have a lower temperature than the other parts of the photosphere. Each sunspot is larger than Earth, and some are thousands of times larger. Sunspots usually occur in pairs or groups. A large sunspot

group may contain dozens of spots and last for several weeks. There is also a cycle of sunspot activity: every twenty-two years the sunspot cycle reaches maximum. The next period of maximum sunspot activity is expected in the year 2012.

When the Sun's surface is active with numerous sunspots, it affects Earth. The increase in solar energy produces a very active corona around the Sun. The **solar wind** from the corona makes Earth's atmosphere glow, causing what is known as the **aurora**.

Sunspots are associated with **solar flares**, which are some of the largest explosions in the solar system. These flares are large clouds of energy that are pushed away from the Sun. One of the largest solar flares ever seen occurred on January 6, 1997. It sent a cloud of high-energy particles racing toward Earth at more than 2.6 million miles

◄

A solar flare erupts thousands of miles into space from the Sun's surface. Sometimes enough energy results from a flare that when it reaches the Earth, it disrupts communications networks and creates the Aurora Borealis, or Northern Lights.

AURORA BOREALIS

The Aurora Borealis is caused by solar energy (solar wind) reacting with the Earth's atmosphere.

Also known as the Northern Lights, the Aurora Borealis is a spectacular atmospheric light show that occurs under the right conditions. First, solar energy is deflected by Earth's magnetic field into our planet's polar regions. These particles add energy to the atmosphere, and when the energy is released, cause different-colored light to dance in the night sky.

(4.6 million km) per hour. These particles slammed into Earth's magnetic field four days later and damaged the electronic equipment on several Earth-orbiting satellites. In general, powerful solar flares can disrupt radio, telephone, and television transmissions.

SOLAR ECLIPSES

A **solar eclipse** occurs when the Moon passes in front of the Sun. If the Moon completely covers the Sun, it is called a **total solar eclipse**. If the Moon just covers part of the Sun, it is called a **partial solar eclipse**. A strange geometry makes eclipses possible: the Moon's diameter is four hundred times smaller than the diameter of the Sun, but the Moon is also over four hundred times closer to Earth. This makes both objects appear the same size in the sky, about 0.5 degree (on a scale of 0 to 360) wide.

▼

This total solar eclipse of the Sun occurred in 1966. The Sun's chromosphere and corona are visible from behind the shadowy disk of the Moon.

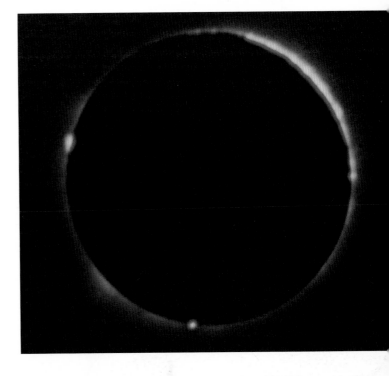

Types of Solar Eclipse

When the Moon passes between the Sun and Earth, it casts a shadow that sometimes falls on Earth. The shadow has two parts: the central dark shadow called the **umbra**, and the lighter shadow called the **penumbra**. A total solar eclipse occurs when the umbra reaches the surface of Earth. In order to see a total solar eclipse, an observer must be in the path of the Moon's shadow, referred to as the **path of totality**. An observer outside this path will see a partial solar eclipse. If the umbra does not reach Earth, the eclipse is called an **annular solar eclipse**; during such an eclipse the Moon's diameter appears smaller than that of the Sun, and a ring of sunlight appears around the dark disk of the Moon. In order to see this type of eclipse, you must also be directly in the path of the umbra, even though the shadow does not fall on Earth. Observers outside of this path see a partial solar eclipse.

Totality refers to the length of time during which the Moon covers the Sun completely. The length of totality can be as short as a second or as long as several minutes. The duration of a total solar eclipse is the result of many variables: the speed at which the Moon's shadow moves across Earth; the point from which the eclipse is observed (important because Earth's rotational speed seems different at different latitudes); how far Earth is from the Sun (this changes because the planet's orbit is elliptical), which alters the perceived diameter of the Sun; and how far the Moon is from Earth (this changes because the Moon also follows an elliptical orbit), which alters the Moon's apparent diameter.

The longest total solar eclipses occur in the sum-

▼
In a solar eclipse the Moon passes between the Earth and the Sun. The darkened lunar disk slowly covers the Sun, a process that is just beginning in this photograph.

▼
During totality the lunar disk completely covers the Sun. A glowing white corona extends thousands of miles in every direction around the Sun. The shape of the corona is influenced by the activity on the Sun's photosphere. Each total solar eclipse produces a slightly different-shaped corona.

mer, with the observer located near Earth's equator at a time when the Moon is closest to Earth on its orbit. The longest any total solar eclipse can last is only 7 minutes 58 seconds.

Special Effects of a Solar Eclipse

Moments before totality the Sun and Moon form what is called the diamond ring, a circle of sunlight, punctuated by a brilliant spike of light that surrounds the Moon's silhouette. At the last seconds this "diamond ring" might break up into beads of sunlight called Baily's beads (named for the nineteenth-century English astronomer who first observed the phenomenon), caused when the mountains and valleys on the Moon's surface break up the edge of the solar image. During totality the harmful energy of the Sun is blocked by the Moon, and observers get a chance to view the outer atmosphere of the Sun, the corona. The corona appears as a glowing

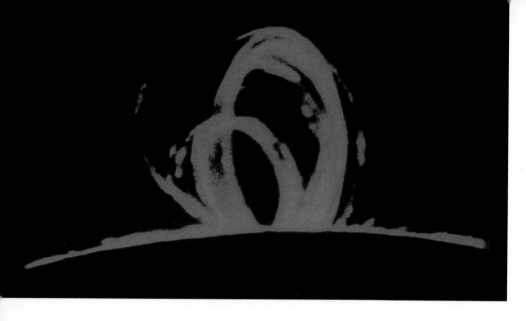

band of light stretching for millions of miles in all directions around the Sun. Along the edge of the lunar disk **prominences** appear as pink hot spots. The moments spent observing a total solar eclipse are very special to astronomers, who travel all over the world to position themselves in the path of totality. Sometimes bad weather prevents scientists from observing an eclipse, but most consider it worth the effort of travel to have a chance of seeing a totally eclipsed Sun.

CALENDAR OF TOTAL SOLAR ECLIPSES FROM 1997 TO 2010

The chance of seeing a total solar eclipse in your own backyard is slim because there are only about fifty total solar eclipses each century. If you could put yourself in the path of totality and observe every total solar eclipse over one hundred years, you would experience fewer than fifty minutes of darkness. The following is a list of the total solar eclipses from 1997 to 2010.

Date	Maximum Totality	Location
March 9, 1997	2 minutes 50 seconds	Siberia
February 26, 1998	4 minutes 8 seconds	South America and Caribbean
August 11, 1999	2 minutes 22 seconds	Europe
June 21, 2001	3 minutes 53 seconds	South Africa
December 4, 2002	2 minutes 3 seconds	Mid-Pacific Ocean
November 23, 2003	1 minute 7 seconds	Antarctic
April 8, 2005	42 seconds	Mid-Pacific Ocean
March 29, 2006	4 minutes 6 seconds	Africa
August 8, 2008	2 minutes 27 seconds	Arctic
July 22, 2009	6 minutes 38 seconds	Eastern Pacific Ocean
July 11, 2010	5 minutes 20 seconds	South Pacific Ocean

COMETS OF OUR SOLAR SYSTEM

The appearance of a **comet** was a terrifying sight to early civilizations. In fact, many people considered them the harbingers of doom. They were thought to bring death and plague to Earth. Today comets are appreciated as cosmic spectacles and are viewed with enthusiasm and wonder. Made of frozen gases and rock, comets are often described as dirty snowballs in space. Specifically, comets are made of carbon monoxide, carbon dioxide, nitrogen, and methane, along with traces of other gases. The dust in a comet is possibly compounds of silicon and oxygen called **silicates**. Astronomers believe that comets are remnants of the original material that formed the solar system.

▼

In this photograph of Halley's comet taken in 1986, a well-formed coma can be seen being pushed back by the solar wind to form a tail more than one million miles (1.6 million km) long.

Periodic Comets and Open Orbit Comets

Some comets travel in elliptical orbits around the Sun. Such comets are referred to as **periodic comets**. A comet's **period** is the time it takes to complete one orbit. There are also comets with orbits that are considered **open**, which means the comets are expected never to return. The orbits of most comets are not on the same orbit plane, or ecliptic **(Vol. 5, p. 35)**, as the planets. Some orbits are almost perpendicular to the orbit plane of the planets, approaching the solar system from above or below the ecliptic. The most famous periodic comet is Halley's comet **(pp. 39–40)**.

Photographed during the evening in March 1976, Comet West can be seen here with a fan-shaped tail trailing out behind it. This event was easily visible to millions of people.

Comet Shoemaker-Levy broke into several pieces before crashing into Jupiter in 1984. It was the first time astronomers had ever seen a comet hit a planet.

The orbits of periodic comets sometimes change as they pass within the gravitational pull of a large planet. The comets' orbits might be altered to such a degree that they are forced out of the solar system, hit a planet, or run into the Sun. In 1994 astronomers were able to witness a comet crashing into a planet when comet Shoemaker-Levy collided with Jupiter. It was the first time anyone had ever witnessed such a collision. Comet Shoemaker-Levy was broken into twenty-one pieces by the gravitational pull of Jupiter before it hit the planet. Some of the resulting explosions on Jupiter were bigger than the planet Earth, and the shock waves rip-

Comet Hale-Bopp (1997) was perhaps the brightest comet to appear in Earth's sky in the past two hundred years. It was photographed in the morning and evening sky for several months as it entered the solar system and headed back into the depths of space.

pled through the giant planet's cloud belts for more than a year **(Vol. 4, pp. 23–24)**. Imagine what would happen if a giant comet hit Earth.

Parts of a Comet

A comet is a frozen object several miles wide. The bright head of the comet is called the **coma**, which is actually a very thin layer of

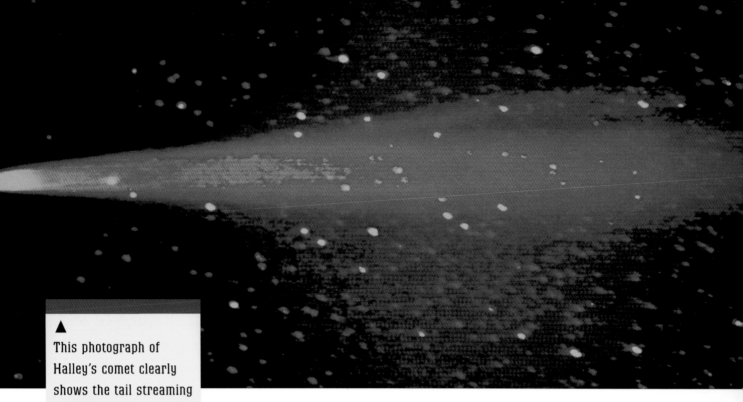

This photograph of Halley's comet clearly shows the tail streaming out more than one million miles (1.6 million km) behind the coma.

gases surrounding the comet. In the center of the coma is a small rock and ice core called the **nucleus**, which is usually only a few miles across. When the comet gets near the Sun, the gases reflect the sunlight, causing the comet to glow. It is at this stage that astronomers usually notice a comet. When the comet gets closer to the Sun, a "tail" appears behind it as the dust and gases are pushed back by the solar wind **(p. 32)**. Comets have two types of tail (though sometimes only one is apparent): gas and dust. The **dust tail** is the brighter, more visible part. Some dust tails appear to be more than one million miles (1.6 million km) long. The **gas tail** appears faint and is usually straighter, as the solar wind easily pushes the low-mass gases directly away from the Sun. A study of the spectra of these tails identifies them as ionized gas and dust particles.

Halley's Comet

English astronomer Edmond Halley (1656–1742) did not discover the comet that bears his name, but he was the first to recognize that it was the same comet returning every few dozen years. Throughout history astronomers have recorded visits of this comet; the first recorded appearance was in 239 B.C. Halley's comet has a period of seventy-six years. On its last visit it came closest to the Sun on February 9, 1986. Scientists got a rare look at Halley's comet that year when the spacecraft Giotto passed within 373 miles (600km) of its core. The nucleus was 9.3 miles (15km) long and roughly 5 miles (8km) wide and has been described as peanut-shaped. Giotto also discovered that almost 80 percent of the material jetting out of the comet's nucleus is water vapor, and 20 percent is dust. The dust was discovered to be mainly carbon

(like pencil lead) with some silicates. The comet will not be visible again in Earth's skies until the year 2061.

Hale-Bopp

A large comet named Hale-Bopp visited our solar system in 1997. Its nucleus was estimated to be 25 miles (40km) wide. Discovered by amateur astronomers Alan Hale and Thomas Bopp in July 1995, it has a period of slightly more than 2,400 years. It first appeared as a brilliant starlike object approaching the Sun, with a tail more than 100 million miles (160 million km) long. Later during its stay it could be observed in the evening sky as it headed back toward the edge of the solar system. Hale-Bopp passed within 1.31 astronomical units (AU) of Earth on March 22. It reached **perihelion** (the point in a celestial object's path when it is closest to the Sun) on April 1 at a distance of 0.94 AU. This comet is one of the brightest to appear in Earth's skies in the past two hundred years.

The Oort Cloud and the Kuiper Belt

Comets are found far away from the Sun in the cold of space. Some astronomers believe that these comets were formed in the **asteroid belt (pp. 46–49)** between Mars and Jupiter, and were pushed away by the gravity of Jupiter. The Dutch astronomer Jan H. Oort (1900–92) suggested that comets come from a cloud of comet material, sometimes known as the Oort Cloud, which is located billions of miles from the Sun. Most comets spend their time in this cloud and are never seen. When a comet is disturbed by the gravity of a passing star or some interstellar event, it falls toward the Sun, creating a cosmic show. In 1951 another belt of comets was discovered just beyond the orbit of Neptune by Dutch astronomer Gerard Kuiper (1905–73). As of this writing, there have been thirty-one objects discovered in the Kuiper Belt. Comets in this part of the solar system have fairly stable orbits, but the gravity of Neptune could make some of them unstable. Some astronomers suggest that the planet Pluto could be a large member of this comet belt.

Comets Visit Earth

The geological record of Earth reveals that our planet has been pounded thousands of times by comets, meteors, and asteroids. Some of these impacts were catastrophic to the planet. For instance, at the end of the **Permian Period** (more than 250 million years ago) a major event of this nature occurred that wiped out 95 percent of all life, including most reptiles, mammals, and plants. Then around 65 million years ago another event occurred that caused an estimated 75 percent of life, including all the dinosaurs, to perish. Geologists Walter and Luis Alvarez speculated that the massive damage to Earth's atmosphere and ecosystem may have been caused by a comet, meteor, or asteroid—weighing 100 million megatons and measuring approximately 6 miles (9.6km) in diameter—that crashed into the planet.

In the late 1970s Walter Alvarez noticed a layer of clay that seemed to separate two geological layers, known as the **Cretaceous-Tertiary (K-T)** boundary. The Cretaceous period ended some 65 million years ago. Walter showed some of this clay material to his father, Luis Alvarez. In this clay layer they discovered a large amount of iridium, a rare **heavy metal** found in abundance in meteorites and, possibly, comets (humans have never obtained comet

This photograph of comet Hale-Bopp was taken in the morning sky in March 1997. The tail of the comet is formed by the solar wind and so always points away from the Sun.

material to study). This element also exists naturally on Earth, but in small amounts. The clay from the K-T boundary contained very large amounts of this element, indicating a global "rain" of iridium dust over Earth. Recent core samples have confirmed traces of iridium-rich material around the globe. This is evidence that something happened during this geological time that changed life on Earth.

Astronomers suggest that Earth could be hit by a comet or other space object at any time. Judging from the past history of Earth and its planetary neighbors, one major impact occurs roughly every 100 million years.

▼
This 1985 photograph shows comet Ikey-Seki.

METEORS OF OUR SOLAR SYSTEM

As it orbits the Sun, Earth travels at an average speed of more than 66,000 miles per hour (106,000km/h), its atmosphere encountering space dust and other debris. Friction usually causes small rocks and dust to vaporize on contact with the molecules of Earth's atmosphere. Observers often see these collisions as streaks of light against the night sky and call them "falling stars" or "shooting stars," which is inaccurate. These objects are actually **meteors**.

Most meteors never reach the surface of the planet. They are traveling so fast that the friction caused by contact with the molecules of Earth's atmosphere heats their outer surface to more than 2,000°F (1,093°C). In a matter of seconds the outer surface of the meteor begins to glow as it quickly burns. Astronomers estimate that each day Earth encounters more than 25 million meteors that burn brightly enough to be visible. On any dark, clear night Earthbound observers should be able to see an average of seven meteors per hour.

Meteor Terminology

A meteor goes through three stages: it is called a **meteoroid** when it is still in space, a meteor when it enters Earth's atmosphere, and a **meteorite** when it hits the planet. It has been estimated that more than 400 billion meteor-like dust particles enter the atmosphere each day. Most of them are too small to be seen. According to some estimations, this dust material adds an additional 100 million tons (91 million metric tons) to Earth's mass each year. That sounds like a lot, but because the planet is so large and because the material is spread over the entire surface of the planet, it is not enough to be noticed.

Meteor Craters

Meteors average in size from grains of sand or marbles to large, building-size objects. Meteors are traveling more than 30 miles per second (48km/s) when they start to encounter air molecules 60 miles (96km) above Earth. If the meteor is small, it will vaporize completely as its surface heats up. Sometimes large meteors do not burn up completely, and crash into our planet. In Quebec, Canada, there is a meteor crater more than 40 miles (64km) wide. Meteor craters on Earth are reminders that the planet has been hit thousands of times by these

▶

Meteor showers appear several times each year. In this engraving the Leonid meteor shower appears to fill the sky with "shooting stars."

rocks from space. Over time there have been more craters on Earth than are currently visible on the surface of the Moon, but most of Earth's craters are gone. Scientists have located around 150 remaining craters worldwide, but many of these craters no longer look much like craters. They have been almost completely washed away by Earth's weather.

The most famous meteor crater on Earth is in Arizona. Measuring 4,100 feet (1,250m) across and 570 feet (174m) deep, it was

◀

This meteor crater in Arizona is the most recent large-impact crater on Earth. It was formed by a large iron-nickel meteor striking the Earth fifty thousand years ago. The crater is nearly 600 feet (182m) deep and more than 4,000 feet (1,216m) wide.

▶
These children were photographed sitting in pits of the Willamette meteorite in the Hayden Planetarium, New York City, in 1939.

caused by a large meteorite weighing millions of tons that hit the planet with such force that it displaced about 300 million tons (272 million metric tons) of rock. The original meteorite exploded into millions of pieces. An estimated 15 tons (13.6 metric tons) of material has been collected at the impact site.

Meteorites from Mars

Recently scientists have been studying several meteorites believed to be from Mars. Astronomers suspect something collided with Mars approximately 600,000 years ago, forcibly catapulting these rocks into space. For thousands of years these rocks spiraled in toward the Sun, and some of them eventually entered Earth's atmosphere and landed on the planet. A few of these were found on the frozen surface of Antarctica. Scientists have been studying a Martian meteorite labeled ALH84001 for clues about possible life on Mars. Inside ALH84001 they found chemical evidence that suggests living things once inhabited the red planet. The study of other Martian meteorites may help solve the mystery of how life began (or evolved) on Earth.

▼
This meteor, known as ALH84001, is believed to have once been part of a 4.5 billion-year-old rock on Mars. It was blasted from Mars more than sixteen million years ago and fell to Earth in Antarctica thirteen thousand years ago. It may contain evidence that primitive organisms once lived on Mars.

Meteor Showers

On certain nights of the year you can see dozens of meteors during **meteor showers**, when the number of meteors that appear per hour increases over the course of several hours or days. The meteors seem to radiate from a point in the stars, so astronomers give the shower the name of the constellation **(Vol. 5, pp. 9–10)** in which the radiant point is located. The meteors are not actually coming from the constellation; they just seem to radiate from that area of the night sky. It is believed that these showers are caused by dust from the orbits of comets. As Earth orbits the Sun, it crosses these dust trails. Several meteor showers are worth noting. The Perseid meteor shower **(Vol. 5, p. 46)** in August usually produces dozens of visible meteors and is perhaps the best shower to observe. The Leonid meteor shower **(Vol. 5, p. 53)** in November is famous for its "meteor storm."

Every thirty-three years the Leonids produce a shower of more than 150,000 meteors per hour. The last time this occurred was in 1966. It is expected to happen again in 1999.

▼ Meteor shower nights offer a chance to view hundreds of meteors. By keeping the shutter open on a tripod-mounted camera, it is possible to take a photograph that shows meteors as streaks of light.

METEOR SHOWERS

Here are some suggested nights for watching meteor showers.

Shower	Dates	Number per hour	Associated Comet
Quadrantids	January 3–4	85	?
Lyrids	April 21–22	15	Thatcher
Eta Aquarids	May 3–5	25	Halley
Delta Aquarids	July 29–30	30	?
Perseids	August 11–12	100	Swift-Tuttle
Orionids	October 20–21	20	Halley
Leonids	November 16–17	12	Temple-Tuttle
Geminids	December 14	95	Asteroid Phaeton

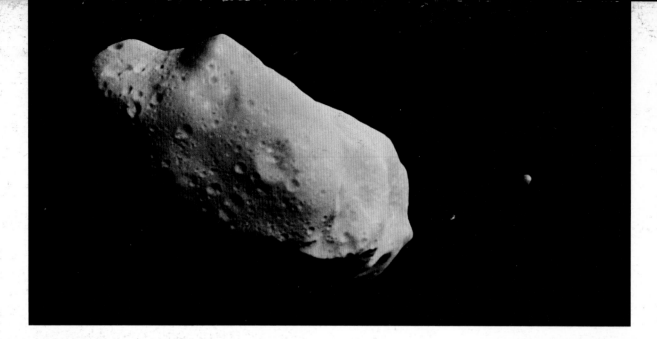

ASTEROIDS OF OUR SOLAR SYSTEM

Orbiting the Sun in the darkness of space are billions of small objects known as **asteroids**, ranging in size from dust specks to mountain-like chunks. Unlike meteors, asteroids travel in regular orbits. Most asteroids orbit between Mars and Jupiter in a zone known as the **asteroid belt**. This belt does not contain much matter overall, perhaps the amount of a small planet, but nonetheless might hold a clue to the birth of our solar system. Astronomers have a theory that asteroids (and meteors and comets) are the original material of the solar system, the rocks and dust that did not coalesce into a single planet. Some suggest that the combined gravity of Jupiter and the Sun may have prevented the forma- tion of a planet in this part of the solar sys- tem. The asteroids orbiting near Jupiter travel erratically, producing many collisions, with the final result of millions of smaller pieces.

Sometimes these collisions force pieces of asteroids to move farther into space, even out of the solar system. Other pieces fall toward the Sun, and some hit the planets. Some large meteorites are possibly pieces of rock from the asteroid belt.

Asteroid Ida was pho- tographed by the Galileo spacecraft on August 28, 1993. The space- craft was 6,500 miles (10,400km) from the asteroid and discovered the asteroid had a moon (visible on the right).

Giant Asteroids

The largest objects in the asteroid belt are sometimes called **minor planets**. Ceres, the largest and the first ever discovered, has an estimated diameter of 596 miles (960km), which makes it about one-third the size of Earth's Moon. Sicilian astronomer Giuseppi Piazzi (1746–1826) discovered Ceres on January 1, 1801. By 1890 more than three hundred asteroids had been found; today there are more than two thousand named

Jupiter

Vesta

Ceres

Hector

Psyche

Eunomia

The asteroid belt is
located between Mars
and Jupiter and contains
millions of asteroids of
all shapes and sizes.
The first asteroid was
discovered in 1801 and
named Ceres. It is 596
miles (960km) in diame-
ter and covered with
craters. Other notable
asteroids are also illus-
trated here.

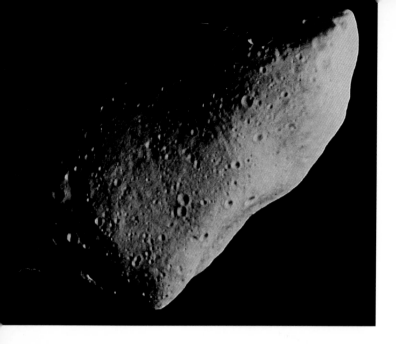

or numbered asteroids, though hundreds of thousands of asteroids may exist in the solar system.

Asteroid Orbits

A few asteroids move in elliptical orbits that cross the orbits of the planets. These asteroids are classified according to their orbit paths. The Mars-crossing asteroids are called **Amor asteroids**. The Earth-crossing are called the **Apollo asteroids**, and the **Aten asteroids** are

THE LARGEST ASTEROIDS

Name	Diameter
Ceres	596 miles (960km)
Pallas	378 miles (608km)
Vesta	345 miles (555km)
Hygeia	280 miles (450km)
Euphrosyne	230 miles (370km)
Interamnia	218 miles (350km)
Davida	200 miles (323km)
Cybele	192 miles (309km)

found inside the orbit of Mars and seem to have left the asteroid belt completely. Some of the Apollo asteroids that cross the orbit of Earth close to the planet are called near-Earth asteroids or **Earth-grazers**. There are more than two hundred known Earth-grazer asteroids. In 1993 a small asteroid measuring 30 feet (9m) across and identified as 1993KA2 "grazed" Earth, passing within 84,000 miles (135,000km) of the planet. It was the closest asteroid encounter ever detected. The first close-up photo of an asteroid was taken in 1992. On its way to Jupiter the spacecraft Galileo photographed the asteroid Gaspra. Almost 12 miles (19km) long and covered with small craters, it may have been chipped off a larger object some 200 million years ago **(Vol. 12, pp. 49–50)**. In 1996 a small spacecraft was launched to intercept the asteroid Eros, which measures 22 miles (34km) in diameter and orbits just outside the orbit of Mars **(Vol. 12, pp. 51–52)**.

Large Asteroids

On November 1, 1977, a strange object was discovered near the orbits of Saturn and Uranus. It was unlike anything seen before in the solar system. Scientists named it Chiron. Its diameter is estimated at 100 miles (161km), and its surface is dark like that of an asteroid. It was moving in a near-circular orbit near Uranus, with a period calculated at 50.7 years.

The scientific community listed it as a minor planet, but in 1988 it suddenly got brighter. Chiron appeared to develop a coma, like a comet. Astronomers now think Chiron might be a giant comet in an orbit much like that of a planet. Saturn's gravity is pulling constantly on Chiron, making its orbit unstable. It might be waiting in the cold of space until the gravity of Saturn directs it out of the solar system, toward the Sun, or possibly toward Earth.

Asteroids Visit Earth

As with giant meteors and comets, large asteroids may have caused major changes on Earth by colliding with the planet, creating gigantic craters and causing long-lasting global damage. There is a good chance that a past major impact may have occurred in one of Earth's oceans, causing a tsunami 800 feet (244m) high and destroying the shoreline around the

ocean basin. It may have been a large asteroid hitting Earth 65 million years ago that caused mass extinctions **(pp. 41–42)**.

Smaller asteroids (or meteors) like the one that may have made the Arizona crater possibly hit Earth every 10,000 to 50,000 years. Astronomers believe that a large asteroid could hit Earth again one day. Some experts estimate the odds at once every 250,000 years; others predict a time span of several million years, and some suggest it might happen any time.

THE OUTER REACHES

The Sun's family stretches far beyond the orbit of Pluto. The Sun's field of gravity reaches billions of miles across the vastness of space. Only four spacecraft have had the

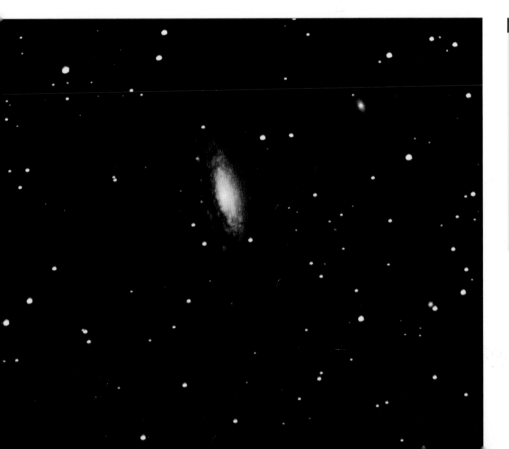

◄

Galaxies such as this one (known as NGC 7331, photographed on April 3, 1978) appear as dense clusters of stars in space. Each galaxy contains millions of stars. Our galaxy is called the Milky Way.

energy to pull completely away from the Sun's gravity. It has been more than a quarter of a century since the Pioneers **(Vol. 4, pp. 11–12; Vol. 12, pp. 52–53)** were launched, and over two decades since the Voyagers **(Vol. 4, pp. 13–14; Vol. 12, pp. 52–53)**. They are still affected by the Sun but are venturing farther from Earth than any other manmade objects in history. While they no longer send back pictures from this distance, they do confirm by weak radio signals that the solar wind reaches billions of miles into space.

Planet X

In the outer reaches of the solar system there could be another planet that no one has yet observed. Any time people search for a new planet in the solar system, the potential planet is referred to as **Planet X**, which is not a name, but a label attached to the hypothetical planet. A planet beyond Pluto might be so distant that it does not reflect much sunlight. Its orbit location might be 5 to 10 billion miles (8 to 16 billion km) from the Sun. Such a planet might take five hundred years to orbit and would not show up on film exposed to the heavens for the expess purpose of detecting the motion of new planets. Many astronomers doubt the existence of any planets so far from the Sun. If a new planet is discovered, though, it will be given the name of a Roman god or goddess, like all the other planets.

The Nemesis Star

Many stars we see in the night sky are **double stars (Vol. 6, p. 21)**. Our Sun could have a companion star, called the **nemesis star**, drifting somewhere in the darkness of space. Though it is now considered unlikely, some people suggest that a small, dark solar companion might be responsible for changes in the orbits of comets, and even for the ice ages on Earth. No such object has been identified as yet.

► This HST photograph of a large spiral galaxy known as Markarian 315 has two nuclei, located approximately 6,000 light years apart. The brighter nucleus is thought to be powered by a massive black hole. The fainter nucleus is considered to be the core of a smaller galaxy that recently merged with the larger spiral.

Future Solar Systems

Gazing deeper into outer space, scientists have located the great clouds of interstellar dust and gas of other nebulae, which are the future star-makers. Many reflect the light from nearby stars, and in some it is possible to observe the dark centers of future solar systems already developing **(Vol. 12, pp. 42–44)**. In the future there will be new stars to gaze upon, and possibly new planets to discover.

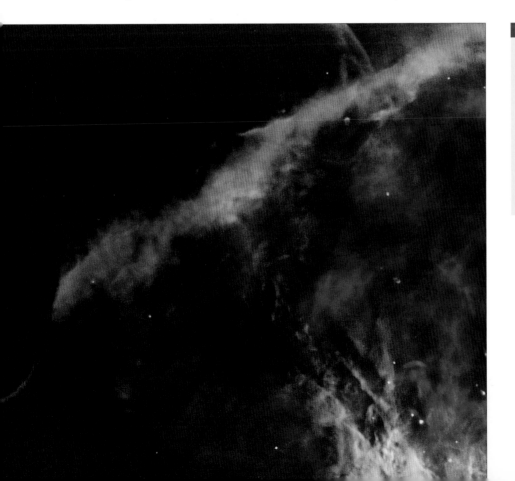

◄ This photograph of the sunset over the South African horizon was taken by the crew of the space shuttle from an altitude of 156 nautical miles (290km).

CONCLUSION

The Sun's family is a small-to-average-size star system in the Milky Way Galaxy. The Sun itself has been radiating energy for billions of years and will continue for at least five billion years into the future. Today we know the Sun's gravity extends far into space and holds dozens of planets, moons, asteroids, and comets in its grasp. The planets and their moons seem peaceful, but their cratered and scarred surfaces reveal a violent history and hold the promise of a similarly tumultuous future. The Sun's family is often visited by cosmic neighbors, as the stars push and pull on interstellar space. We are sometimes treated to the celestial fireworks of solar eclipses, meteor showers, and passing comets.

If our solar system represents a typical star with planets, what will other solar systems be like? Future astronomers will solve some of the mysteries but will also undoubtedly raise new questions for future generations.

This HST photograph
from 1991 shows a
mosaic image of a small
portion of the Orion
Nebula. New features
that were revealed by
this photograph include
rapidly expanding
plumes of material
around young stars and
protoplanetary disks.

GLOSSARY

Absolute zero The temperature at which a substance possesses no heat energy: -459.67°F (-273.15°C)

Ammonia A colorless gas used to manufacture nitrogen-containing organic and inorganic chemicals

Amor asteroids Group of asteroids moving in elliptical orbits that cross the orbit of the planet Mars

Annular solar eclipse A solar eclipse in which the Moon's umbral shadow does not reach Earth. Observers see a ring of sunlight around the dark lunar disk

Apollo asteroids Group of asteroids traveling in elliptical orbits that cross the orbit of planet Earth

Asteroid belt A grouping of asteroids orbiting the Sun, located between the orbits of the planets Mars and Jupiter

Aten asteroid Group of asteroids orbiting inside the orbit of the planet Mars

Atmosphere The gaseous mass surrounding a celestial body, especially Earth, which is retained by the celestial body's gravitational field

Axis of rotation An imaginary straight line (which on a planet is drawn through the poles) about which a body rotates

Black dwarf The final stage of a star that has exhausted all of its energy into space

Centrifugal force apparent force on a body in curvilinear (circular) motion, which is directed away from the center of curvature, or the axis, of rotation

Chromosphere One of the three main divisions of the Sun's observable outer gaseous layers, the others being the photosphere and the corona

Coma In comets it is the luminous gaseous envelope surrounding the nucleus and forming the head of the comet

Constellation Eighty-eight official patterns of stars in the night sky forming the shapes of animals and objects.

Corona A faint halo of highly ionized gas outside the chromosphere of the Sun

Crater A bowl-shaped depression in the surface made by a volcano or an explosion or the impact of a body such as an asteroid or meteorite

Dust tail The bright tail of a comet, which consists mostly of dust and water vapor pushed back from the comet's nucleus by the solar wind

Earth-grazers The term given to celestial objects that pass close to planet Earth, such as asteroids and meteoroids

Eclipse In astronomy when one object blocks the light of the other. In a solar eclipse the Moon passes in front of the Sun. In a lunar eclipse the Moon passes into the Earth's shadow

Ecliptic The plane of the solar system, or the apparent yearly path of the Sun against the celestial sphere as seen from Earth

Electromagnetic energy Wavelength energy, including heat, X-rays, cosmic rays, gamma rays, ultraviolet, infrared, microwaves, and the visible spectrum

Ellipse A slightly flattened circle

Erosion Natural processes—including weathering, abrasion and corrosion—by which a planet's surface is worn away

Gas tail Comet tail composed mainly of gases. Appears in photographs of comets as straight when compared to the dust tail, which may be curved or fan shaped

Geocentric Having the Earth as the center. Many early astronomers thought the Earth was at the center of the universe, with the Sun, Moon, and planets revolving about it in circular orbits

Gravitational collapse The movement of matter by gravity toward the center of attraction, such as the collapse of a nebula or star

Gravity The universal attraction between all objects having mass

Helium An odorless, gaseous element occurring in natural gas. Two hydrogen atoms fuse together to form helium in the nuclear reactions that take place inside the Sun

High-pressure area Region on the surface of a planet, such as Earth, where the air pressure is above the average air pressure

Hydrogen A colorless, flammable gaseous element that is the most abundant element in the universe and the main fuel of the stars

Infrared Wave energy longer than red and below the visible spectrum. Used in radio astronomy and in remote controls.

Ionized Describing atoms that have been converted into ions (groups of atoms that have a positive or negative charge)

Jovian planets Term given to planets similar to Jupiter, that is, planets that appear to be made mostly of gases

Magnetic field A detectable, attractive force found at every point in the region of a magnet or electric current, and extending between a planet's magnetic poles

Mass The amount of matter an object contains. The mass of the body is not dependent on gravity, and is therefore different from, but proportional to, its weight

Meteorite A meteor that strikes the surface of a celestial body, for instance Earth

Meteoroid A stony or metallic mass of matter found in space similar to asteroids but usually smaller

Meteor shower A visual display caused by many meteorites entering a planet's atmosphere

Methane An odorless, colorless flammable gas commonly used as a fuel that is also an important source of hydrogen and other organic compounds

Nebula A cloud of interstellar gas and dust that reflects or absorbs light; where stars are born

Nitrogen A nonmetallic, odorless, colorless element that constitutes nearly four fifths the Earth's atmosphere

Noble metal A term for such metals as gold and silver that do not corrode or deteriorate rapidly

Nuclear fusion The release of energy from matter by the joining of the nuclei of lighter elements to make heavier ones; the combined mass is less than that of the parts, and the difference is released as energy

Nucleus The central part of the head of a comet, usually a frozen ball of ice, dust, and rock

Occult When one celestial body passes in front of another, as when a planet or moon passes in front of a distant star

Open orbit An orbit that appears to be so large that it might possibly be open at one end, indicating that the object will never return; typical of many comet orbits

Orbit The path an object follows around another due to the gravitational force between them

Oxygen A nonmetallic element that constitutes 21 percent of Earth's atmosphere. It is essential for life as it exists on Earth

Partial solar eclipse An eclipse of the Sun viewed from outside the path of totality, in which the Moon does not appear to completely cover the solar disk

Path of totality The path—usually 125 miles (201km) wide and 2,000 miles (3,218km) long—taken by the Moon's shadow across Earth's surface during an eclipse

Penumbra The area of partial shadow between the umbral shadow and the area of complete illumination

Perihelion The point closest to the Sun reached during an object's orbit of the Sun

Period The amount of time it takes a celestial body to complete one orbit

Photons A stable, positively charged subatomic particle found in the nucleus of an atom

Photosphere The visible surface of the Sun. It is made of gases and gives off energy

Prominence A bright cloud of gases arcing off the Sun's photosphere into space

Radar imaging A process in which the images are captured by the use of radar waves instead of visible light

Rotate The turning of a body, such as a planet, on its axis

Silicates Numerous compounds containing silicon, oxygen, and metals; more than 90 percent of the Earth's crust is composed of two kinds of silicate

Solar flare A burst of energy in the photosphere of the Sun. Associated with prominences, solar flares stimulate the active solar wind

Solar granules The ricelike appearance of the photosphere that is due to the convection currents in the Sun's gases

Solar wind The energy streaming in all directions from the Sun's photosphere

Sunspot Dark spots associated with magnetic storms on the Sun's photosphere, these regions have a lower temperature. They usually occur in cycles of twenty-two years

Totality The time during a solar eclipse when the Sun is completely hidden by the Moon or in a lunar eclipse when the Moon is completely covered by Earth's shadow

Total solar eclipse A solar eclipse in which the Moon completely occludes the Sun

Ultraviolet rays Energy of a shorter wavelength than the visible blue wavelengths of the electromagnetic spectrum

Umbra The darkest part of a shadow or sunspot

Visible spectrum The rainbow of colors we see in the Sun's light. Red has the longest visible wavelength and violet has the shortest visible wavelength

Wavelength The distance between one peak, or crest, of a wave energy, such as light, and the next corresponding peak. Short wavelengths appear blue and longer wavelengths appear red

White dwarf A low luminosity star of small size and great density in the later stages of its life cycle

SET INDEX

Volume numbers appear in **bold**. Page references in *italics* refer to pages with photographs and illustrations.

A

Aldrin, Edwin "Buzz," **2:** 47; **8:** 36, 40, 41; **9:** 6, 26; **10:** 6, *7*
Aliens, **6:** 47
Allen, Joseph, **9:** *40*
Alpha Centauri, **6:** 17, 18; **7:** 50
Anders, William, **2:** 46; **8:** 38; **10:** *8*
Apollo spacecraft, **2:** 9, 28, *31*, 43–51; **8:** *6,* 32, *33, 40;* **9:** 6, 8; **10:** 7, *30,* 31, *32*
Armstrong, Neil, **2:** 46, 47; **8:** 36, 40, 41; **9:** 6, 26; **10:** *6–7*
Asteroids, **1:** 7, 46–49; **2:** 11, 31; **3:** 46; **4:** 13, 31, 52; **7:** 11, 21; **8:** 51, 52; **12:** 49–52
Astronauts, **2:** *14,* 43, 46, 47, 48, 50; **8:** 26, 27, *28,* 30, *33, 35,* 38; **9:** 6, 26, *28,* 36, *40–41, 44–46, 48, 50,* 52; **11:** *7, 20–22,* 26, *30, 31, 37, 39,* 42
   commanders, **10:** 15–16
   early, **10:** 9–11
   mission specialists, **10:** 15, 17
   moon landings, **10:** 6
   payload specialists, **9:** 51; **10:** 15, 18
   pilots, **10:** 15, 16
   selection process, **10:** 12–15
   training, **10:** 6, 7, 19–21
Astronomers, **6:** 7; **7:** 8–10, 13–15, 17–21
   amateur, **7:** 21
   in education, **7:** 20
   radio, **7:** 18
   research, **7:** 18
   theoretical, **7:** 20
Astronomical units (AU), **1:** 27, 40; **3:** 33; **6:** 17; **8:** 15
Astronomy, **11:** 6
   ancient, **7:** 8–10
   early, **5:** 12–14
   modern, **5:** 14–15
   radio, **7:** 34–36
   satellites, **7:** 45–49
Astrophysics, **7:** 17, 21

Atlantis shuttle, **9:** *7, 23,* 26, *32, 43,* 49; **10:** 24; **11:** *38,* 39
Atlas spacecraft, **10:** 11
Auroras, **1:** 32, *33;* **4:** 24

B

Bean, Alan L., **2:** 48; **11:** *23*
Belayev, Pavel I., **8:** 30
"Big Bang," **6:** 41, 48; **7:** 48, 49
Black holes, **6:** 13, *27,* 28–29, 31, 46, *47,* 49; **7:** 20; **12:** 43
Borman, Frank, **2:** 46; **8:** 38; **10:** *8*
Brahe, Tycho, **1:** *13,* 14; **2:** 36, 42; **5:** 15
Brilliant Pebbles program, **12:** 47
Bursch, Daniel, **10:** *46*

C

Cabana, Robert, **9:** *41*
Caisson's disease, **10:** 35
Calendars, **2:** 18; **5:** 12; **7:** 9
Cameron, Kenneth, **10:** *8, 16*
Cape Canaveral Space Center (Florida), **2:** 44; **8:** *14;* **9:** *16,* 17
Carpenter, Scott, **8:** *29;* **10:** *12*
Carr, Gerald, **11:***24*
Cassini probe, **4:** *14,* 15, 39; **8:** 52, *53;* **12:** 13, 47
Challenger shuttle, **9:** *13,* 26, *29,* 34, *35, 42,* 47
Chilton, Kevin, **9:** *32;* **11:** *31*
Clementine probe, **12:** 47, 48
Clifford, Michael, **9:** 41; **10:** *7;* **11:** 31
Collins, Michael, **2:** 47; **8:** 36, 40, 41; **9:** 26; **10:** 6, 7
Columbia shuttle, **9:** *6–7, 14–16,* 22, *24,* 26, *32, 37;* **10:** 16, *47;* **12:** *42*
Comets, **1:** 7, 37–42; **2:** 11; **4:** 35, *52, 53;* **5:** 26; **6:** 30; **7:** 21, 40; **8:** 51, 52; **12:** 49–52
   Giacobini-Zinner, **12:** 51
   Grigg-Skjellerup, **12:** 51
   Hale-Bopp, **1:** *38,* 40, *41;* **7:** 52–53
   Halley's, **1:** *37, 39–40;* **3:** 31; **7:** *46;* **8:** 51; **12:** 51
   Hyakutake, **2:** *50;* **12:** 50
   Ikey-Seki, **1:** *42*
   IRAS-Araki-Alcock, **7:** 46
   Kohoutek, **11:** 24
   open orbit, **1:** 37
   parts, **1:** 38–39

   periodic, **1:** 37, 38
   Shoemaker-Levy, **1:** *38;* **4:** *23–24;* **7:** 37, 40, 42
   West, **1:** *37*
Conrad, Charles Jr., **2:** *14, 47,* 48; **10:** 41; **11:** *7, 20, 22*
Constellations, **5:** 6, 9–10; **6:** 11, 15; **7:** 6
   Aquarius, **7:** *44*
   Aquila, **5:** 42–43
   Auriga, **5:** 28
   Big Dipper, **5:** 32–33
   Boötes, **5:** 37–38
   Canis Major, **5:** *29,* 30
   Canis Minor, **5:** *30*
   Cassiopeia, **5:** 47–48
   Centaurus, **11:** 33
   Cepheus, **5:** 48–49
   Cetus, **5:** 52
   Cygnus, **1:** 11; **5:** 40–41; **7:** *47;* **11:** 33–34
   Draco, **5:** 35
   Gemini, **5:** *31,* 32
   Hercules, **5:** 45–46
   Leo, **5:** 35–37
   Little Dipper, **5:** 33–34
   Lyra, **5:** 39–40
   Ophiuchus, **5:** 44
   Orion, **1:** *11;* **5:** *23,* 24–25; **6:** 15; **7:** 42
   Pegasus, **1:** 11; **5:** 50–51
   Perseus, **5:** 52–53
   Pisces, **5:** 51–52
   Sagittarius, **5:** 43–44; **6:** 40; **7:** 34
   Scorpius, **5:** 43
   Serpens, **5:** 44–45
   Sirius, **7:** 50
   Taurus, **5:** *27,* 28; **6:** 26
   Triangulum, **6:** 39, *43*
   Ursa Major, **1:** 11; **5:** *32,* 33
   Ursa Minor, **5:** 33–34
   Vela, **11:** 33
   Virgo, **1:** 11; **5:** 38–39
Cooper, Gordon, **10:** *12*
Cooper, Leroy Jr., **8:** *29*
Copernicus, Nicolas, **2:** 36; **5:** *14,* 15; **7:** 13, 14
Copernicus spacecraft, **12:** 43
Cosmonauts, **2:** 43; **8:** 23, 30, 33; **11:** *7,* 9, *15,* 26, *27, 30,* 31, *32–33, 35,* 36, *37, 39,* 42
   early, **10:** 9–11
   selection process, **10:** 13–15
   training, **10:** 21–22
Crippen, Robert, **9:** *32*

synchronous rotation, **2:** 22, *23,* 24

terrain, **2:** *7–8, 11,* 13, *28–29;* **5:** *18,* 19

tidal friction, **2:** 17

Multi-Object Spectrometer, **9:** 47

Musgrave, F. Storey, **9:** *44–45*

N

NASA. *See* National Aeronautics and Space Administration

National Aeronautics and Space Administration, **3:** 50; **8:** 52; **9:** 15; **10:** 7, 9, 15, 16, 17; **11:** 11, 18, 42, 48; **12:** 36, 39, 44, 47, 51, 52

Near-Earth Rendezvous spacecraft, **12:** 51, 52

Near-Infrared Camera, **9:** 47; **12:** 41–42

Nebulae, **1:** *8,* 10–11; **2:** 9; **5:** 6, 7; **6:** *17,* 19, 23, 30, 40; **7:** 25, 42

absorption, **5:** 25

Bridal Veil, **6:** *35*

Cat's Eye, **7:** *39*

dark, **5:** 25; **6:** 33, 35

diffuse, **6:** 33

emission, **6:** 32–33

Horsehead, **5:** *25*

Lagoon, **5:** *44*

North American, **1:** *11*

Orion, **1:** *11, 53;* **5:** 8, *25;* **7:** 39

Pelican, **6:** *34*

planetary, **6:** 25, *32;* **7:** 39

reflection, **6:** 33

Nelson, George, **10:** *17*

Neptune, **1:** 14; **4:** 6, 45–48; **7:** 12, 39, 40, 50–51

atmosphere, **4:** 46–47

color, **1:** *25*

composition, **4:** 46–47

Great Dark Spot, **4:** *46,* 47

missions to, **4:** 13, 14; **8:** 51–52; **12:** 8, 52

moons, **4:** 8, 47–48

observing, **4:** 10–11

orbit, **1:** 25

period, **4:** 8

ring system, **4:** 47

rotation, **4:** 8

storms on, **7:** 40

temperature, **1:** 25

terrain, **3:** 19

Newman, James, **10:** *51*

Newton, Isaac, **5:** *19;* **7:** 20, 30; **12:** 9, 15

North Star, **3:** 35, 36; **7:** 22

O

Observatories, **3:** *48*

ancient, **7:** *9,* 22

Egyptian, **7:** 9, 22

Keck (Hawaii), **7:** *33*

Lick, **7:** 30

Mauna Kea (Hawaii), **7:** *25, 36,* 45

Mayan, **7:** 9, 22

McDonald Observatory (Texas), **7:** 22

modern, **7:** 22

permanent, **7:** 22

side-by-side, **7:** 33

Stonehenge (England), **5:** *11;* **7:** 22

United States Naval Observatory (Washington), **7:** 25

Yerkes (Wisconsin), **7:** 25

Ochoa, Ellen, **10:** *17*

Onufrienko, Yuri, **11:** *27, 32, 35, 39*

Oort Cloud, **1:** 40; **4:** 53; **6:** 30

Orbits, **12:** 7

asteroid, **1:** 48

elliptical, **2:** 19; **8:** 7; **12:** 15

geosynchronous, **9:** 42; **12:** 31–33

Moon/Earth, **2:** 17–18

outer planets, **4:** *9*

planetary, **1:** 12–15

satellites, **12:** 22–23

solar, **12:** 46

speeds, **1:** 13–14

tilts, **1:** 12–13

velocity in, **8:** 14

P

Pioneer spacecraft, **1:** *7;* **3:** 14, 31; **4:** 11, 13, *19,* 37; **8:** 32, 48, *51;* **12:** *9,* 46, 53

Planetariums, **7:** 20

Planets, **1:** 9

atmosphere, **8:** 11

densities, **4:** 7

diameters, **4:** 8

distances to, **3:** 18

formation of, **7:** 42–43

inferior, **3:** 11

inner, **3:** 6–52; **4:** 6

Jovian, **4:** 6, 7

moons, **4:** 8

motion of, **7:** 12,13

orbits, **1:** 12–15; **3:** 10; **8:** 7

outer, **1:** 21–26; **4:** 6–55; **7:** *12,* 39

periods, **4:** 7–8

proplyds, **7:** 42

retrograde motion, **5:** 14; **7:** 12–13

rotation, **4:** 7–8

superior, **3:** 11

temperatures, **4:** 7

terrestrial, **1:** 16–20; **3:** 19; **4:** 6

volcanic activity on, **3:** 20; **7:** 40

Plate tectonics, **3:** 19, 30, 37; **4:** 29

Pluto, **1:** 14; **4:** 6–7, 49–51; **7:** 12, 42, 50

composition, **4:** 50

missions to, **4:** 13

moons, **4:** 8, *49,* 50–51; **7:** 42

observing, **4:** 10–11

period, **4:** 8

rotation, **1:** 26; **4:** 8

Pluto Express, **4:** 15; **7:** 42

Pogue, William, **11:** *24*

Polyakov, Valery, **10:** 14; **11:** 26

Popovich, Pavel, **10:** 13

Progress spacecraft, **11:** 16, 28, 31, 33

Proton rockets, **11:** 15

Protoplanetary disks, **7:** 42

Protostars, **7:** 42

Ptolemy, Claudius, **2:** 38; **5:** 14; **7:** 12–13

Pulsars, **5:** 28; **6:** 26–27; **12:** 43, 53

Q

Quasars, **6:** 13, *44–45, 46, 47*

R

Radiation, **6:** 7; **7:** 16. *See also* Rays and waves

atmospheric, **8:** 21

background, **7:** 48–49

cosmic, **11:** 10, 45

electromagnetic, **6:** 27; **7:** 50; **12:** 42

high-energy, **7:** 47–48

infrared, **6:** 13; **12:** 41–42

ultraviolet, **6:** 13; **12:** 43

Ranger spacecraft, **2:** 42; **8:** 32

Rays and waves. *See also* Light

gamma, **7:** 8, 45, 47; **12:** 42

infrared, **7:** 16, 38, 45; **11:** 33

light, **7:** 17, 45

microwave, **7:** 16–17, 45, 48–49

energy production, **1**: 9, 28

gravity on, **1**: 6, 8–9, 14

layers, **1**: 29–31; **6**: 10

mass, **1**: 10, 27

observing, **11**: 18, 22, 25

size of, **7**: 15

sunspots on, **1**: 32

surface, **1**: 6, *27*

temperature, **1**: 32; **6**: 8

Supernova, **5**: 15, 28; **6**: 25–26, 37; **11**: 34

Surveyor spacecraft, **8**: 32

Swigert, John, **2**: *48;* **8**: 43

T

Taurus, **6**: 26

Telescopes, **7**: 8, *14, 22, 23;* **10**: 11; **12**: 25

aerial, **7**: *7*

anatomy of, **7**: 26–28

Cassegrain, **7**: *26, 32, 33*

coudé focus, **7**: *32, 33*

early, **7**: 14

Hooker, **7**: 25

Hubble Space Telescope, **1**: 8, 26; **4**: 7; **6**: 41; **7**: 18, *24,* 37–44, 47; **9**: 44–47; **12**: *39–40,* 41, 49

infrared, **6**: 27

New Technology Telescope, **7**: 33

Newtonian, **7**: 30, *31,–32*

optical, **7**: 18, 26–33

prime focus, **7**: 30, *32*

radio, **6**: 13, 27, 40, 44, 46; **7**: *18,* 34–36

reflecting, **5**: *19;* **7**: 26, *28, 30,* 37

refracting, **7**: 25, 26, *28*

solar, **11**: *21,* 25

Uhuru, **12**: 43

ultraviolet, **11**: 33; **12**: 42

Very Large Array (New Mexico), **7**: 35–36; **12**: *13*

X-ray, **6**: 27; **11**: 33

Telstar satellite, **12**: 32

Tereshkova, Valentina, **8**: 25; **10**: *13, 18*

Theory of relativity, **1**: 28; **7**: 20; **12**: 21

Thornton, Kathryn, **10**: *43*

Titan-Centaur rockets, **8**: *50*

Titan rockets, **2**: 44; **8**: 17

Titov, Gherman, **10**: 11, *13*

Tombaugh, Clyde, **4**: 49, 52–53

Truly, Richard, **9**: *36*

U

UFOs, **6**: 48

Ulysses spacecraft, **9**: 49; **12**: 44, *45, 46*

Universe

age of, **7**: 44

closed, **6**: 49

end of, **6**: 48–49

flat, **6**: 49

geocentric view, **1**: 12; **5**: 13–14; **7**: 10, 12

heliocentric view, **3**: 10; **5**: 14–15, 17, *18;* **7**: 13–15

open, **6**: 49

size of, **7**: 15, 44

structure of, **7**: 20

Uranus, **1**: 14; **4**: 6, 40–44; **7**: 12, 39, 50

atmosphere, **1**: 24; **4**: 41–42

color, **1**: *24*

composition, **4**: 41–42

missions to, **4**: 13–14; **8**: 51–52; **12**: 8, 52

moons, **4**: 8, *43–44*

observing, **4**: 10–11

orbit, **1**: 25

period, **4**: 8

ring system, **1**: 23; **4**: *42*

rotation, **1**: 24; **4**: 8

terrain, **3**: 19

Usachev, Yuri, **11**: *27, 35,* 39

V

Vacuums, **8**: 16; **11**: 18

Van Allen, James, **8**: 21

Van Allen belt, **8**: 23

Vanguard satellites, **8**: 22–23

Vega, **6**: *12*

Vega spacecraft, **3**: 31

Vela, **11**: 33

Velocity, **8**: 11

Venera spacecraft, **3**: 27, 31

VentureStar, **9**: 53

Venus, **1**: 14, *17;* **3**: 25–31; **7**: 50

atmosphere, **1**: 17; **3**: 9, 14, *25, 27*

diameter, **3**: 26

distance to, **3**: 26

gravity on, **3**: 19

magnetic field, **3**: 30

maps of, **3**: *28*

missions to, **3**: 12; **8**: 48–50; **12**: 50

observing, **3**: 9–11, 14

rotation, **3**: 26

size, **3**: 25

storms on, **3**: 27

temperature, **1**: 17; **3**: 27

terrain, **1**: *18;* **3**: 6, 19, 28–30

volcanoes on, **3**: *20,* 26, *29,* 30, *31*

Viking spacecraft, **1**: 20; **3**: 16, 18, 46–47, 49; **8**: 49, *50*

von Braun, Wernher, **11**: *11*

Voskhod spacecraft, **8**: *31*

Voss, Janice, **10**: *50*

Vostok spacecraft, **8**: 23, *24–25,* 29–30, *31;* **10**: 11

Voyager spacecraft, **4**: 13–14, 18, 20, 22, 30, 37, 42, 47–48; **6**: 18; **7**: 40, 51; **8**: 12, *13,* 51; **12**: 8, 46, *53*

W

Waves. *See* Rays and waves

Weightlessness, **8**: 7–8, 28; **10**: 20, 26–30; **11**: 11, 34, 49; **12**: 11

Weitz, Paul, **11**: *7, 20, 23*

White, Edward H., **8**: 34, *35;* **10**: *11*

Wide-Field Planetary Camera, **9**: 47–48; **12**: 41

X

X-Ray Multi-Mirror Mission (XMM), **12**: 43

X-Ray Timing Explorer (XTE), **12**: 43

Y

Young, John, **2**: 46, 49; **9**: *32*

Z

Zodiac, **5**: 32; **7**: 10

Zond spacecraft, **8**: 32